A Woman's Blueprint for a Godly Marriage
Written under the inspiration of the Holy Ghost
Garrick and Dannielle

A book for every Woman & any inspiring soul.
For a Blessed, Full, Content, Happy, Joyful & Peaceful
Life; with the desires of your heart being fulfilled.

"Delight yourself in the LORD.
And He will give you the desires of your heart."
(Psalm 37:4 NASB)

Chapters:

1) Blessings of the Blueprint
2) The Fraudulent and Deceptive Blueprint
3) The Collapse of Not Following the Blueprint
4) The Blueprint of Christ and his Church/Bride
5) The Great General Contractor/Spirit
6) The Uneducated and Unlearned Novis "Way of man"/ "Heart of man"
7) The Disappointments and Failures
8) The Rebuilding with the Accreted Blueprint
9) The Peace, Joy and Contentment

Introduction

To all that read this book: I pray that the spirit of God will lead and bring revelation that you may know what the mind of the spirit is. I also pray that faith will abound in your hearts. The things I am going to talk about and the things my wife is going to speak of are spiritual and need to be looked at in the that light because it says, "But a natural man does not accept the things of the Spirit of God, for they are foolishness to him; and he cannot understand them, because they are spiritually discerned. But he who is spiritual examines and judges all things, yet he himself is judged by no one. For WHO HAS KNOWN THE MIND OF THE LORD, THAT HE WILL INSTRUCT HIM? But we have the mind of Christ." [1Co 2:14-16 NASB]

Be careful not to view these things from the thoughts of man or this world because they will be foolishness. Even as people tried to hear what Christ was saying and became offended; "Trust in the LORD with all your heart and do not lean on your own understanding. In all your ways acknowledge Him, And He will make your paths straight. Do not be wise in your own eyes; Fear the LORD and turn away from evil. It will be healing to your body and refreshment to your bones. Honor the LORD from your wealth and from the first of all your produce; So, your barns will be filled with plenty and your vats will overflow with new wine. My son, do not reject the discipline of the LORD Or loathe His reproof, For whom the LORD loves He reproves, even as a father [corrects] the son in whom he delights. How blessed is the man who finds wisdom and the man who gains understanding. For her profit is better than the profit of silver and her gain better than fine gold. She is more precious than jewels; And nothing you desire compares with her." [Pro 3:5-15 NASB]

"It is the Spirit who gives life; the flesh profits nothing; the words that I have spoken to you are spirit and are life. [John 6:63 NASB]

"But an hour is coming, and now is, when the true worshipers will worship the Father in spirit and truth; for such people the Father seeks to be His worshipers. God is spirit, and those who worship Him must worship in spirit and truth." [John 4:23-24 NASB]

Intro-Dannielle

Garrick and I have been married now for over 15 years, by God's grace! We have had a lot of struggles, but the key has always been keeping God the center of our life. With each day serving the Lord, he has caused us to change and grow individually with our relationships with him. Through our own personal relationships with God and being renewed in his sprit daily we have grown together as husband and wife by his spirit we have been united. There were many unnecessary struggles I had as a wife because I kicked against the pricks! I somehow thought I knew better than God (Foolish, I know!). I did not fully surrender to the blueprint as the word of God lays out. Despite my foolishness God has continued to show me his ways which are truly life, peace and joy forevermore. My desire is that my life would be an example to women of faith, that through sharing my testimony women might gain the wisdom and understanding God has revealed to me. My hope is for women with an ear to hear that you might take heed and therefore be blessed in abundance and use my mistakes as fuel to your fire of what NOT to do in your relationship with the husband that God is going to give you. Trust me ladies, taking the hard road and fighting against God just makes your life miserable. There are very shameful things I said and things I did that were completely opposite the blueprint of God, but by God's tender mercies he has chosen to open my eyes and remove the vail. I believe that even in the majority of churches today the true way God lays out for women and wife's is twisted. We have power as women when we follow God's way and that comes through prayer. We must be lead of the spirit of God if we truly want to have life in abundance. I encourage every woman reading this book to keep your hearts open to receive the true promises and blessings of God for your life, that he would grant your eyes to see and ears to hear his truth. You must be honest with yourself about your shortcomings and do not try to cover them up or hide. As God reveals things to you that are in your heart, I encourage you to keep a humble and meek spirit. Just remember that God will use your husband to revel and teach you many things as that is his job.

"There is a way which seemeth right unto a man, but the end thereof are the ways of death." (Proverbs 14:12 KJV)

"Confess [your] Faults one to another, and pray one for the another, that ye may be healed. The effectual fervent prayer of a righteous man availeth much." (James 5:16)

"But he giveth more grace. Wherefore he saith, God resisteth the proud, but giveth grace unto the humble." (James 4:6)

"Pride [goeth] before destruction, and an haughty spirit before a fall." (Proverbs 16:18)

"But [let it be] the hidden man of the heart, in that which is not corruptible, [even the ornament] of a meek and quiet spirit, which is in the sight of God of great price." (1 Peter 3:4)

Chapter 1: Blessings of the Blueprint

1. Comfort
2. Peace
3. Joy
4. Contentment
5. Love
6. Intimacy
7. Friendship
8. Safety
9. Rest
10. Fulfillment
11. Satisfaction
12. A clean continence
13. Health
14. Provision
15. Happiness

With me having two wife's I can tell you firsthand that one of them Embraced it with many struggles but has always seen God's grace and help. I saw her continually mature in the Lord. I have also seen a wife start a good path forward growing and doing good. I then saw her completely turning from God and going the other direction, throwing his words behind her back. In Psalms 50 it talks of people that want to live wicked and what God will do to them and its very fearful or Hebrews 10:26-31 [Heb 10:26-31 KJV] 26 For if we sin willfully after that we have received the knowledge of the truth, there remaineth no more sacrifice for sins, 27 But a certain fearful looking for of judgment and fiery indignation, which shall devour the adversaries. 28 He that despised Moses' law died without mercy under two or three witnesses: 29 Of how much sorer punishment, suppose ye, shall he be thought worthy, who hath trodden under foot the Son of God, and hath counted the blood of the covenant, wherewith he was sanctified, an unholy thing, and hath done despite unto the Spirit of grace? 30 For we know him that hath said, Vengeance [belongeth] unto me, I will recompense, saith the Lord. And again, The Lord shall judge his people. 31 [It is] a fearful thing to fall into the hands of the living God.

Remember the goodness and the severity of God for our God is a God to be feared!

With all your getting it says to get wisdom and understanding and bind them on your neck. In such a time as we live in, we can see so much failure because God's way is disregarded and distained. If you desire life and blessings grab hold of God's blueprint. Don't delay; embrace with your whole heart, mind, body and soul the teaching of our heavenly father so you may have life more abundantly!

"For to be carnally minded [is] death; but to be spiritually minded [is] life and peace." (Rom 8:6 KJV)

God, the father, has a blueprint and if it is followed it shall bless you beyond all you can think or imagine. God's ways are perfect. Our father, God wants good for his children. God is for us and as a good father when we are not following his directions, he is faithful to bring a loving correction.

"For whom the LORD loves He reproves, even as a father [corrects] the son in whom he delights." (Pro 3:12 NASB)

"And you have forgotten the exhortation which is addressed to you as sons, "MY SON, DO NOT REGARD LIGHTLY THE DISCIPLINE OF THE LORD, NOR FAINT WHEN YOU ARE REPROVED BY HIM;
FOR THOSE WHOM THE LORD LOVES HE DISCIPLINES, AND HE SCOURGES EVERY SON WHOM HE RECEIVES." It is for discipline that you endure; God deals with you as with sons; for what son is there whom [his] father does not discipline? But if you are without discipline, of which all have become partakers, then you are illegitimate children and not sons. Furthermore, we had earthly fathers to discipline us, and we respected them; shall we not much rather be subject to the Father of spirits, and live? For they disciplined us for a short time as seemed best to them, but He [disciplines us] for [our] good, so that we may share His holiness. All discipline for the moment seems not to be joyful, but sorrowful; yet to those who have been trained by it, afterwards it yields the peaceful fruit of

righteousness. Therefore, strengthen the hands that are weak and the knees that are feeble," (Heb 12:5-12 NASB)

Remember there is hope if you are out of alignment of following the father's blueprint. Just humble yourself under the mighty hand of the father and Christ Jesus, your husband and he will raise you up. Don't be proud, for then God shall resist you. Following the true blueprint will produce the good fruit, which is love, joy, peace, patience, kindness, goodness, faithfulness, gentleness, self-control and against these things there is no law.

You'll become free when you lose your life and die to yourself then the fruit of the spirit grows in you, it will cause you to become free and causes you to be good and pleasing to Christ and will be a rich blessing to your husband.

Blueprints are useful for the result of everything in your life being blessed. If a woman follows the blueprint she shall succeed in her marriage and be blessed. Now if a woman is being abused, she is free to separate and should because Christ Jesus our good husband treats us with the upmost love even laying his life down for us. If a woman us being cheated on she does not need to stay in that relationship unless she directly hears God say stay but if she is in harm in any way she should leave.

"But I say to you that everyone who divorces his wife, except for [the] reason of unchastity, makes her commit adultery; and whoever marries a divorced woman commits adultery."
(Matthew 5:32 NASB)

Have you ever had food where someone left out a key ingredient? Like a cake without the sugar or say you get a vanilla latte, and you take a sip and realize that they left out the vanilla. When you just leave out even one ingredient it makes for a big letdown. Just like not following the blueprint of God precisely. God is not mocked if you deviate and do not follow His plan it surely shall bring heart ache. Let these things settle into the heart and remember God's ways are higher than your ways and will lead to life and peace.

Chapter 1-Dannielle

I am reminded of the story of Queen Ester, one of my favorite stories in the Bible. Before Ester could be Queen, Queen Vashti had to fulfill her purpose. She was given a position as Queen and with that came a blueprint to follow. Queens could not act on their own authority. Queen Vashti was an example to all the women of the Persian nation of how NOT to live. King Ahasuerus summons her to come before him to his banquet or party. He wanted to show her beauty off to his people, but Vashti refuses the King. This angers King Ahasuerus. Memucan, a prince of Persia suggests that the King make a commandment that Queen Vashti come no more before the King.

"For the queen's conduct will become known to all the women causing them to look with contempt on their husbands by saying, 'King Ahasuerus commanded Queen Vashti to be brought in to his presence, but she did not come.' (Esther 1: 17 NASB)

This is a realization here! Queen Vashti was not right in her heart. She thought she had some power to do her own thing. She was not in subjection unto her King. If we as women of God do not want to submit to the authority God puts over us God most certainly can strip us of our position. He can take our blessings and promises and give them to someone else. Our husbands are the authority God put over us, if we as women of God don't want to submit to this order God can most certainly strip us of our positions.

"But as the church is subject to Christ, so also the wives ought to be to their husbands in everything." (Ephesians 5:24 NASB)

There have been quite a few tests God brought to me, trying my obedience to my husband Garrick. Each time I failed a test God's peace and comfort would leave me and fear and dread would fall upon me. This is his tender mercies to us that He does not leave us in our iniquity and sin but says here is the way out, grab hold of me! God is no respecter of persons. Just as we saw this with queen Vashti being removed from her position.

"Therefore humble yourselves under the mighty hand of God, that He may exalt you at the proper time,
casting all your anxiety on Him, because He cares for you. Be of sober *spirit,* be on the alert. Your adversary, the devil, prowls around like a roaring lion, seeking someone to devour. But resist him,
firm in *your* faith, knowing that the same experiences of suffering are being accomplished by your brethren who are in the world. After you have suffered for a
little while, the God of all grace, who called you to His eternal glory in Christ, will
Himself perfect, confirm, strengthen *and* establish you. To Him *be* dominion forever and ever. Amen." (1 Peter 5:6-11 NASB)

Just as Prince Memucan ends his advice to King Ahasuerus, saying to give Queen Vashti's royal estate to a woman better than her. The King was pleased with the princes' words, and he sent out a royal commandment to every province.

"When the king's edict which he will make is heard throughout all his kingdom, great as it is, then all women will give honor to their husbands, great and small." (Esther 1:20 NASB)

The key here is being in subjection or submission to the king of kings. Remember we are daughters of the Most High. We have a requirement as serving God of how we are to be. We are to be lights in darkness. We are to stand out from the women of this earth. We should most certainly be different from the way worldly women act and behave to their husbands. We as Christian women should set a clear example.

For so long I had this twisted thought process. I thought how can I submit myself to my husband. He is just a man. He makes mistakes just like I do. He is in this flesh too. How is he any better than me? Let me point out all of these are accusations, and we know that the devil is the accuser of the brethren. Not to mention that none of these thoughts reflect the truth that God has laid out as our blueprint in his word as the blueprint for our life's. This whole thought process I had gave into fed the ways of the world and the devil. Remember every single thought comes from either God or the Devil. There is only good and evil. The thoughts we think and feed in our minds become who we serve.

"No one can serve two masters; for either he will hate the one and love the other, or he will be devoted to one and despise the other. You cannot serve God and wealth." (Matthew 6:24 NASB)

One day God spoke to me and said, "Your life is not your own! You serve me alone. I bought you with the blood of my son. I gave you your husband and I can take him away if you do not want to honor him as I command of you." Now it took me many trials of my faith for this to sink in. I hate to admit but I am a stubborn woman. Unfortunately, I did not walk in humility. I still somehow thought there must be a different way then following a man!

"But He gives a greater grace. Therefore *it* says, "G<small>OD IS OPPOSED TO THE PROUD, BUT GIVES GRACE TO THE HUMBLE."</small> Submit therefore to God. Resist the devil and he will flee from you. Draw near to God and He will draw near to you. Cleanse your hands, you sinners; and purify your hearts, you double-minded. Be miserable and mourn and weep; let your laughter be turned into mourning and your joy to gloom. Humble yourselves in the presence of the Lord, and He will exalt you." (James 4:6-10 NASB)

"For he saith to Moses, "I will have mercy on whom I will have mercy, and I will have compassion on whom I will have compassion." (Romans 9:15 KJV)

"Behold, we count them happy which endure. Ye have heard of the patience of Job, and have seen the end of the Lord; that the Lord is very pitiful, and of tender mercy." (James 5:11 KJV)

"I returned, and saw under the sun, that the race is not to the swift, nor the battle to the strong, neither yet bread to the wise, nor yet riches to men of understanding, nor yet favor to men of skill; but time and chance happeneth to them all." (Ecclesiastes 9:11 KJV)

Chapter:2

The Fraudulent and Deceptive Blueprint

Garrick

Let us remember the children of God are traveling through this life looking for a city whose builder and maker is God. We are looking for a kingdom that lasts forever and we are not of this world. We can see that there's a lot of other blueprints that are contrary to God's blueprint. They all seem to have some sort of higher wisdom and a promise of something thing that is better than God's ways. Just as the serpent from the beginning was a liar and does not support God's blueprint. The devil told eve there was a better way and to not follow God's blueprint and gave a so-called better way, but we can see this led to failure and destruction by following the deceptive suggestions of the Devil. It is no doubt in our societies there rises all types of different doctrines/blueprints with such appealing ideas that bring forth such pleasure, such pride, arrogancy, strife and destruction. On the outside it seems so beautiful and sweet just as the fruit did to Eve. Think on this: the devil is not stupid; he uses things that to our carnal mind are appealing and seem like a great thing, they seem like something wise and of great understanding, something hidden and now you are better than others because you have a special knowledge. Remember all the scriptures are for our learning. It will not end well to not follow God's plans.

"Behold then the kindness and severity of God; to those who fell, severity, but to you, God's kindness, if you continue in His kindness; otherwise

you also will be cut off."
(Rom 11:22 NASB)

We have thousands of years of seeing deception upon deceptions entering the thoughts of man which are contrary to Christ teaching's, they all ended up causing such pain and destruction. Don't be surprised, God has allowed all these things so we must be strong and courageous to maintain doing good and grabbing hold of God's perfect plan. Don't be deceived by their empty talk or flatteries, it always comes with promises of such good things but in their heart, they are slaves to sin, and their minds are darkened by the God of this world. There is only one way to freedom, this is Christ Jesus. As He says I am the way the truth and life. Whoever the son makes free is free indeed. True freedom only comes from Christ Jesus and His blueprint.

Let us read 2 Peter Chapter 2. This chapter is not often talked about in our society as we have promoted the feel-good Jesus and truly he is, but he has other areas of his nature also. We can never come to eternal life unless you know him as he truly is, in the full and entirety of His whole nature. This is eternal life that you know Jesus Christ and the father.

"But false prophets also arose among the people, just as there will also be false teachers among you, who will secretly introduce destructive heresies, even denying the Master who bought them, bringing swift destruction upon themselves. Many will follow their sensuality, and because of them the way of the truth will be maligned; and in [their] greed they will exploit you with false words; their judgment from long ago is not idle, and their destruction is not asleep. For if God did not spare angels when they sinned, but cast them into hell and committed them to pits of darkness, reserved for judgment; and did not spare the ancient world, but preserved Noah, a preacher of righteousness, with seven others, when He brought a flood upon the world of the ungodly; and [if] He condemned the cities of Sodom and Gomorrah to destruction by reducing [them] to ashes, having made them an example to those who would live ungodly [lives] thereafter; and [if] He rescued righteous Lot, oppressed by the sensual conduct of unprincipled men (for by what he saw and heard [that] righteous man, while living among them, felt [his] righteous soul tormented day after day by [their] lawless deeds), [then] the Lord knows how to rescue the godly from temptation, and to keep the unrighteous under punishment for the day of judgment, and especially those who indulge the flesh in [its] corrupt desires and despise authority. Daring, self-willed, they do not tremble when they revile angelic majesties, whereas angels who are greater in might and power do not bring a reviling judgment against them before the Lord. But these, like unreasoning animals, born as creatures of instinct to be captured and killed, reviling where they have no knowledge, will in the destruction of those creatures also be destroyed, suffering wrong as the wages of doing wrong. They count it a pleasure to revel in the daytime. They are stains and blemishes, reveling in their deceptions, as they carouse with you, having eyes full of adultery that never cease from sin, enticing unstable souls, having a heart trained in greed, accursed children; forsaking the right way, they have gone astray, having followed the way of Balaam, the [son] of Beor, who loved the wages of unrighteousness; but he received a rebuke for his own transgression, [for] a mute donkey, speaking with a voice of a man, restrained the madness of the prophet. These are springs without water and mists driven by a storm, for whom the black darkness has been reserved. For speaking out arrogant [words] of vanity they entice by fleshly desires, by sensuality, those who barely escape from the ones who live in error, promising them freedom while they themselves are slaves of corruption; for by what a man is overcome, by this he is enslaved. For if, after they have escaped the defilements of the world by the knowledge of the Lord and Savior Jesus Christ, they are again entangled in them and are overcome, the last state has become worse for them than the first. For it would be better for them not to have known the way of righteousness, than having known it, to turn away from the holy commandment handed on to them. It has happened to them according to the true proverb, "A DOG RETURNS TO ITS OWN VOMIT," and, "A sow, after washing, [returns] to wallowing in the mire." (2Pe 2:1-22 NASB)

Look at verse 1-3; we can see the hearts of people and lots of times they look good on the outward, like such clean nice people, but they are wolves in sheep's clothing. They also may even have huge respect among other people. The religious Leaders in Jesus' day were powerful elite scholars praying all the time and always seemed good on the outside just as so many religious people do in today's day.

Satan transforms/disguises himself as an angel of light and no doubt his children are ministers of righteousness. These people have evil hearts that twist, add or take away from our heavenly father's blueprint. I challenge you to study for yourselves with a good and honest heart before God to know what the good and acceptable and perfect will of our father is and not be conformed to this world and its ways.

Now in verse 4-9 we see our God is to be feared and reverenced in all. It's not a light thing to just follow a belief system but to make full sure that it lines up with the word of God. Be careful because these false teachers will use certain scriptures to build whole foundations of a belief systems but are twisted to look so righteous. They usually puff you up and seem to have some private insight that others don't have. But you have no need for anyone to teach you but the holy spirit will teach you because the word of God is of no private interpretation. Remember Gods word used in its fullness will lead to a clear interpretation not by using a small section. I do want you to know that there are people that God does use to help his people and bring forth teachings and prophesy, but they will lead by example and the Holy Spirit will bear witness to their teaching or prophesies.

Now in verse 10-22 these scriptures explain what type of people they are and there's a lot of these people and groups. They are greedy and love to flatter people, they do not know Jesus Christ or the father. They do not follow our father or our good shepherd. Their father is Satan, and they cannot help but to do his will but like Jesus said my sheep hear my voice and a stranger they won't listen to. Remember daily we must die to the world and its ways. We must be renewed in the inner man which is created after the image/mind of Christ Jesus.

In conclusion we must strive and fight the good fight of faith to prove what the good and acceptable will of God is. Paul told the people don't even believe an angel that preaches some other message. I challenge you to study these things to make sure you are not living in a deception of a different blueprint, so that you can truly build through Christ and the spirit a beautiful building that is built upon the chief corner stone/Christ. Remember he was rejected by the religious people of His day so you may end up not being liked by them or you may already be hated or spoken of evil of but remember they already did this to your Master Jesus. Don't be surprised because it is not only given to you to believe but to suffer for the name of Christ.

Chapter 2-Dannielle

I feel I need to share a prophesy given to my husband and I. We had moved from Wisconsin back to Garrick's hometown of Buena Vista, Colorado. It was a life changing decision for us to move across country with our two sons. We did not attend church for nearly a year after moving. Deciding to move was not something we took lightly. Garrick and I prayed and fasted about making this move. In the end we had no doubts this was what we needed to do. However, the year plus that followed before we moved proved to be one of our biggest trials of our faith. We received such judgement and hate from the church we were attending. I had grown up at this church since I was a baby. We were so heartbroken that fellow believers, that "loved" us could say such cruel things, when all we were doing was following what God spoke to us. After all weren't we supposed to seek God and be lead of him and have our own relationships with him. This did not shake our faith in God but ultimately strengthened our faith.

"In this you greatly rejoice, even though now for a little while, if necessary, you have been distressed by various trials, so that the proof of your faith, being more precious than gold which is perishable, even though tested by fire, may be found to result in praise and glory and honor at the revelation of Jesus Christ; and though you have not seen Him, you love Him, and though you do not see him now, but believe in Him, you greatly rejoice with hoy inexpressible and full of glory, obtaining as the outcome of your faith the salvation of your souls." (1Peter 1:6-9 NASB)

It more made us question how the churches were being lead and taught. About a year after we moved, we started going to church again. There was a man that came as a guest speaker and prophet. Let's just say that hearing these words was truly life changing. At first these words made me angry. I thought how could this man speak these things to me. He doesn't know me. He is way off. I was defensive. I was bitter. I did not have an ear to hear at the time.

"Garrick and Dannielle, okay and children father we ask you to bless come on y'all, bless Garrick and Dannielle, father Lord they have been struggling Lord there's needs and God in the name of Jesus I am asking you for their sake to send angels of provision angels that gather and bring in provision Lord. Angels father that supply needs at your command and father I ask Lord that you would move in their life to bring peace and harmony because it hasn't been harmonious. Father, I ask in the name of Jesus that the peace of God would rule in the heart and home Lord for their sake and their children's sake and for your name's sake and father in the name of Jesus we ask it. Garrick you have been struggling big time and the Lord says you need to call on me. Jeremiah 33:3, I believe it is "call on me and I will show you great and mighty things you know not. That is not just an occasional when your in a bind cry out to God that's a that's is a prayer habit as it were daily going before the Lord, Lord I need your help I need your grace I need your provision I need your blessings okay get in God's face as it were not in a negative way but in an adoring way and tell God just how much you care for him and how much you need him and God says I'll come through for you all right the Lord says I have deliberately allowed you to be put in a tight place to get you to call on me to get you to cry out to me I want a closer relationship with you is what the Lord is saying you see I have a purpose in your life I know you have many obligations and there is only so much time you can dedicate but there is time you can dedicate alright and commit and the Lord says I want that time because I have a purpose cause I want to use you says the Lord I want to bring you to the place that I take your burdens cause I have burdens to give you. You understand that. Lord says I've called you to minister. You're not your own I bought you with the blood of my son says God and God says son I want you to be active in the father's business. And you can't do it burdened down I understand that, but you can begin the preparation process, alright. And it starts with a relationship with God where you hear my voice on a daily basis where you spend time with me, and I spend time with you and out of that will grow the wisdom and knowledge and blessings that's required to begin to lift this burden so that you can carry mine says the Lord. Not that I ever overburden people that's not me when you see people overburdened, they made the choices I didn't put it on them alright so the Lord remember what the Lord says my yoke is easy and my burden is light. He meant what he said he does not overburden people. So, when people are overburdened, it means they've accepted responsibilities and obligations that God didn't necessarily even want them to have. Okay? And the Lord's not telling you that you've done that but what he is explaining to you is the concept that he wants you to be free so that you can do kingdom business says the Lord. Alright? You're going to write books one day by the anointing of God and the grace of God. I have written ten and you're looking at a guy that barely got out of high school. Alright? Never dreamed I would write a book, but the holy spirit already knew upfront okay. So, he's the one that's blessed me to be able to write books, even a best seller nationwide. Now what the Lord's telling you is this it's not the ability you think you have or don't have it is my ability in you. Alright? But you're not free, okay? and you're not going to get free until you recognize that there isn't but one way to freedom and that's God. And the closer I get to God the closer he's going to get to me and the more I am going to be blessed the less I'll have to peruse the blessings the less I'll have to worry about where the moneys coming from and the helps coming from because God will provide it freely and abundantly. And I'll be free to do the masters business says the Lord. So far so good? Okay? Alright? Not a bad deal really if you think it through. Alright, now Dannielle, Dannielle the Lord says in the word of God when I made Adam, I looked at him and said now he's got a pretty good-sized job here I mean the whole worlds at his command he's responsible for it he's going to need some help, so I made Eve. Well Eve didn't do what she was supposed to do. Instead of helping him (hahah) you remember that? She didn't really do what I put her on the earth for. She caused some problems. Now it was his fault he didn't have to obey and submit but nevertheless he did. But her mistake was when she began to operate in her own authority instead of being too submissive to her husband's authority because the first thing, I said to Adam was why did you hearken to your wife. I gave you the authority, but you didn't exercise it. Okay, I am not fussing at you I just telling you what the Bible really says okay Now that gives us a pattern cause when its talking about divorce Jesus says that's not the way it was in the beginning so the way it was in the very beginning that's the way God wants it now and that's where the blessings come in so the more you catch on to that and the more you willingly submit the more Gods going to bless your relationship. And the strive will leave and the discontent will leave the provision will come the blessings will be there the joy and the happiness will be there the meeting of needs the friendship companionship all that will come into its proper place as God ordained it in the beginning, but it won't happen unless we do it by God's pattern instead of our own. Okay? Just a word of ammunition if you will catch on to it, you'll be blessed."

Thankfully (I can say that now!) we had recorded the prophesy. These words have become of such great value to me. These words came directly from the Lord. The Lord knows our hearts. He came to change us. Change is not easy but the results of God purifying us is to come up higher with Him, to grow deeper in love with him.

"The heart is more deceitful than all else And is desperately sick; Who can understand it? I, the LORD, search the heart, I test the mind, Even to give to each man according to his ways, According to the results of his deeds." (Jeremiah 17:9-10 NASB)

Hearing this prophesy began a few years of God working through my husband and through my prayers to root out deeply planted ways of thinking in my heart and mind that were contrary to the word of God for a woman. I am a stubborn woman. Now each part of our characters and how God made us can be used for righteousness or for evil. This was the beginning of the revelation to me that I was being stubborn for the wrong master, and it was wreaking havoc on my life and all those around me.

"But store up for yourselves treasures in heaven, where neither moth nor rust destroys, and where thieves do not break in or steal; for where your treasure is there will your heart be also. The eye is the lamp of the body; so then if your eye is clear, your whole body will be full of light. But if your eye is bad, your whole body will be full of darkness. If then the light that is in you is darkness, how great is the darkness! No one can serve two masters; for either he will hate the one and love the other, or he will be devoted to one and despise the other. You cannot serve God and wealth." (Matthew 6:20-24 NASB)

34

Chapter 3: The Collapse of not Following the Blueprint

Now let's focus on the results of not following the blueprint:

1. Failure
2. Disappointment
3. Heartache
4. Un-contentment
5. Doubt
6. Chaos
7. Double Mindedness – "thinking there's is a better way"
8. Opening Yourself to the Lies and Deceptions of the World and Devil
9. Unstable and Insecure
10. Dirty and Unclean Conscience
11. Blindness
12. Becoming Wretched and Poor Spiritually

Now we must look at the reason man fails. God wants all the glory, honor and praise because He is our Creator and maker, He has ordained all things according to His own will and has written the end from the beginning. God has made mankind and made them to think that they know the way that is right, but God says that the way that man thinks will only lead to death, destruction, and failure.

There is a way [which seems] right to a man, but its end is the way of death. (Pro 14:12 NASB)

Here's an example of this teaching: Jesus says to some people why do you call Me good, there is none good but my Father God. Here's the son of God declaring that he is no good, but his Father is good. If Christ Jesus thought this way, then we as his bride/children are called to walk and think like him as Christ pleased the father, we want to please Christ our Lord. We can read about thousands of years, people and nations that went against and did not follow the blueprint. We see all the trouble that came about from not following God's blueprint.

I also have seen both of my wife's not follow His blueprint, one of them will be the first to admit it and tell you about the suffering it caused her and her family. I also can say that one of my other wife's turned and trampled the blood of Christ under her foot and I weep for her because

God is not mocked, whatever you sow you will reap. In the Bible we can clearly see and have seen thousands of years of people that disregard God, and it has never ended well. I also thank God for his everlasting mercy in that he is not willing that any perish but that we would come to a change of heart and mind that we would live. If you are debating following the blueprint, don't! Remember God is love so all his ways and commandments are pure and true love. I saw firsthand the hurts and disappointments my wife would go through not following God's plan for her life and Gods blueprint. I saw the doubts which caused her to be tossed around like a rag doll, not knowing what to think or believe. She was hearing God then hearing the Devil and the mindset of the world. I would see her feel and embrace the spirit of God and see such peace, love and joy start to flow. Then all the sudden the voice of the enemy would enter the mind and trick her into believing it was her thoughts. She would believe and confess then the chaos would rise like tornado in the mind and in her actions. It would bring such sorrow, such contempt and so much disappointment. Then all she could see was negativity/darkness about herself, me and her life. It would suck all the joy peace and happiness right out of her and cause such pain to her, me and our children. Then I would see her go talk to God and He would talk to her, and she would come and say sorry to me and the children for all the things she would say and do, and we would forgive her. Then out of the ashes she would slowly get back up and walk in the spirit and follow God's ways. Here's a bit of wisdom: the devil is a liar from the beginning and does not abide in the truth. He comes to people and speaks lies but uses so called false truths. Here's an example God showed me: Imagine you and a friend go to the store your friend grabs a tomato and during checkout the cashier asks your friend how much per pound the tomato was, and your friend says 45 cents a pound. You were there and saw the sign and it said 95 cents a pound then a voice comes and uses this truth to accuse your friend and says look at your friend she/he is a liar and a cheat. But your friend by accident looked at the sign right by the one for the tomato's which was actually for the cucumber, and it did say 45 cents. So, in your friend's head there was no evil or lying. Here's a couple of scriptures.

"Every good thing given, and every perfect gift is from above, coming down from the Father of lights, with whom there is no variation or shifting shadow." (Jas 1:17 NASB)

"But if you have bitter jealousy and selfish ambition in your heart, do not be arrogant and [so] lie against the truth. This wisdom is not that which comes down from above, but is earthly, natural, demonic. For where jealousy and selfish ambition exist, there is disorder and every evil thing.
But the wisdom from above is first pure, then peaceable, gentle, reasonable, full of mercy and good fruits, unwavering, without hypocrisy." (Jas 3:14-17 NASB)

Here's some other wisdom to fight against, the deception of the enemy. Remember you cannot go off the appearance of things or just thoughts. You must discern how the thoughts that are coming to your mind are making you feel and if they match what comes from the father or from the flesh and the devil. Remember the father's gifts and word are sure and strait forward. Remember the wisdom from above is pure, gentle, peaceable, reasonable, its full of mercy and good fruits, unwavering, without hypocrisy and makes peace, its kind and gives feeling of cleanness and pureness and is beyond anything you will feel from the world. If it causes strife, bitterness, jealousy, selfishness, confusion, debating, hate, just a gross feeling it's from the earth and is devilish.

"Wisdom shouts in the street, she lifts her voice in the square; At the head of the noisy [streets] she cries out; At the entrance of the gates in the city she utters her sayings: "How long, O naive ones, will you love being simple-minded? And scoffers delight themselves in scoffing and fools hate knowledge? "Turn to my reproof, Behold, I will pour out my spirit on you; I will make my words known to you. "Because I called and you refused, I stretched out my hand and no one paid attention; And you neglected all my counsel and did not want my reproof; I will also laugh at your calamity; I will mock when your dread comes, When your dread comes like a storm and your calamity comes like a whirlwind, when distress and anguish come upon you. "Then they will call on me, but I will not answer; They will seek me diligently but they will not find me, Because they hated knowledge and did not choose the fear of the LORD. "They would not accept my counsel, they spurned all my reproof. "So they shall eat of the fruit of their own way and be satiated with their own devices. "For the waywardness of the naive will kill them, And the complacency of fools will destroy them. "But he who listens to me shall live securely and will be at ease from the dread of evil." [Pro 1:20-33 NASB]

    As we look at these Proverbs, we are given insight into the consequences of not listening and following God's blueprint and the results are terrible. Don't let yourself be deceived, for the enemy will surely come and say things like:
    "How do you know God is true?"
    "That's for back then!"

"Do you really need to do all God wants?"
"That was for back when men just ruled over woman."
"Women are just as good as men!"
"You don't need a man to tell you what to do!"
"Men need help, they just don't understand you!"
"You have a better understanding, God showed you!"

But all these things cause you to bypass and usurp your authority and now you become the authority. It's similar to when sin started in Satan, he thought he was better than God/Christ, but it wasn't given to him by God to be called God and have that authority. We can see all this wisdom is not the wisdom from above, it is anti-God's blueprint. Remember this wisdom plays on mankind making them right in their own eyes which will lead unto death, it is earthly and devilish, which leads to doubtful questions and curses. Remember his ways are higher than our ways. In this next chapter we discuss Christ Jesus, his Church and his blueprint.

Chapter 3: Dannielle

Through many trials of my faith, I have come to understand that the voice of the Lord is still and small. The voice of the devil is loud and obnoxious. Think if a person in a crowd is speaking in a normal voice and another person is yelling. Which person will your attention be drawn to?

Like the woman with the issue of blood. She reaches out and touches the hem of Jesus' garment. There was something different in her touch, amongst a crowd of people. Jesus asks his disciples, "Who touched My garments?" They respond saying, "you see the crowd pressing in on You, and You say, 'Who touched Me?' Things are always different when the Lord speaks or moves with his spirit. We just need to listen. I pray that the Lord would give women in this time an ear to hear him. In a time when so many other voices are speaking of what a woman should be, the ONLY voice we want echoing in our ears is the voice of the Lord. Search for his voice, in the midst of all the noise. He will show you the way.

We must realize that there is only one of two master's that we can serve. There is good and evil, there is God and the devil. There are two paths that we can follow in life; there is the straight and narrow path which leads to life (God) and the wide and broad path which leads to death (devil). This seems so simple, yet I believe many people struggle with this and do not realize it. I struggled with this for way too many years. It's like in the cartoons where an angel is on one shoulder and the devil on the other shoulder and they are both speaking into your ear and they are always contrary to each other opposing voices.

"If it is disagreeable in you sight to serve the LORD, choose for yourselves today whom you will serve: whether the gods which your fathers served which were beyond the River, or the gods of the Amorites in whose land you are living; but as for me and my house, we will serve the LORD." (Joshua 24:15 NASB)

"Do not store up for yourselves treasures on earth, where moth and rust destroy, and where thieves break in and steal. But store up for yourselves treasures in heaven, where neither moth nor rust destroys, and where thieves do not break in or steal; for where your treasure is, there your heart will be also. The eye is the lamp of the body; so then if your eye is clear, your whole body will be full of light. But if your eye is bad, your whole body will be full of darkness. If then the light that is in you is darkness, how great is the darkness! No one can serve two masters; for either he will hate the one and love the other, or he will be devoted to the one and despise the other. You cannot serve God and wealth." (Matthew 6:19-24 KJV)

When I look back on the tests God brought to me that ended up being arguments/fights with my husband I realized a common factor. I would meditate on the situation and be talking to God about where I went wrong afterwards. One day, not to long ago I remember sitting and thinking back on a situation where I messed up royally. That is one thing about me I tend to go all or nothing. When I mess up, I do a top-notch job! Anyway, God had spoken to me clearly in the middle of my anger and frustration. It was right before I acted or spoke anything. His voice had been firm and quiet but now sitting here in my prayer closet it was like he reminded me of His voice and those words he spoke. In this moment of clarity, amid my prayer and my mind being focused on Christ alone the voice became all I heard. The peripheral light bulb went off or more like twenty of them all at once! I thought to myself, Dannielle this is it, this is where you're going wrong. There is so much power in what we feed. You must be quick to hear and slow to speak. You must realize where the feelings and emotions are coming from and where they will lead you. In that moment I first heard the Lord's voice, but I had dismissed it like a fly. You are so used to just inadvertently swatting the fly away you do it without thought. I had not even noticed the voice of the Lord in the heat of my anger. I had been so used to reacting this way it was part of my nature. The key when we realize these things and God shows us and brings light to what's in our hearts and what needs changed that we walk in humbleness and humility by surrendering all to him. We are all on a journey of perfection. It is a daily walk with the Lord and being renewed in His spirit daily. Remember you will mess up. How do you proceed after the error?

"Pride comes before a fall but a broken and contrite heart he will not despise." (Psalm 51:17)

It is in the brokenness where God is molding and making us. His discipline is his love for us as his daughters.

"My son, do not reject the discipline of the LORD Or loathe His reproof, For whom the LORD loves He reproves, Even as a father corrects the son I whom he delights." (Proverbs 3:11-12 NASB) "and you have forgotten the exhortation which is addressed to you as sons, "MY SON, DO NOT REGARD LIGHTLY THE DISCIPLINE OF THE LORD, NOR FAINT WHEN YOU ARE REPROVED BY HIM; FOR THOSE WHOM THE LORD LOVES HE DISCIPLINES, AND HE SCOURAGES EVERY SON WHOM HE RECEIVES." It is for discipline that you endure; God deals with you as with sons; for what son is there whom his father does not discipline? But if you are without discipline, of which all have become partakers, then you are illegitimate children and not sons. Furthermore, we had earthly fathers to discipline us, and we respected them; shall we not much rather be subject to the Father of sprits, and live? For they disciplined us for a short time as seemed best to them, but He disciplines us for our good, so that we may share His holiness. All discipline for the moment seems not to be joyful, but sorrowful; yet to those who have been trained by it, afterwards it yields the peaceful fruit of righteousness." (Hebrews 12:5-11 NASB)

"But the one who endures to the end, he will be saved." (Matthew 24:13 NASB)

Chapter 4: Blueprint of Christ/Husband and his Church/Bride

God's wisdom has always been crying out to man, and some have grabbed hold of it. Just as God came to Moses and showed him how it was in the heavenly. He had Moses replicate it on earth. But as we see Moses was chosen of God to show a reflection, a shadow of the heavenly realm and what God did during that time was glorious and so amazing. Now that Christ Jesus, the son of God appeared unto man, he was not showing the reflection or a shadow any longer. Christ was showing us the image of God, he was the living word of God incarnated. God in the flesh declaring the kingdom and what was truly pleasing to God. Here's a scripture I would like us to look at:

"The God who made the world and all things in it, since He is Lord of heaven and earth, does not dwell in temples made with hands; nor is He served by human hands, as though He needed anything, since He Himself gives to all [people] life and breath and all things; and He made from one [man] every nation of mankind to live on all the face of the earth, having determined [their] appointed times and the boundaries of their habitation, that they would seek God, if perhaps they might grope for Him and find Him, though He is not far from each one of us; for in Him we live and move and exist, as even some of your own poets have said, 'For we also are His children.'
"Being then the children of God, we ought not to think that the Divine Nature is like gold or silver or stone, an image formed by the art and thought of man. "Therefore having overlooked the times of ignorance, God is now declaring to

men that all [people] everywhere should repent,"(Act 17:24-30 NASB)

"Or do you not know that your body is a temple of the Holy Spirit who is in you, whom you have from God, and that you are not your own?" (1Co 6:19 NASB)

"Or what agreement has the temple of God with idols? For we are the temple of the living God; just as God said, "I WILL DWELL IN THEM AND WALK AMONG THEM; AND I WILL BE THEIR GOD, AND THEY SHALL BE MY PEOPLE." (2Co 6:16 NASB)

So, we can see that all humans live and breathe and have there being in God as the universe is in him. We also see that he has chosen some people to dwell in, as Christ Jesus said that you must be born of water and the Spirit of God. God does not dwell in everyone, but everyone dwells in him. When you are born of spirit you are now one with God the Father and Jesus Christ, you were bought by the blood of Christ. You are His bride.

These scriptures will set the stage for this next chapter:

"Wives, [be subject] to your own husbands, as to the Lord. For the husband is the head of the wife, as Christ also is the head of the church, He Himself [being] the Savior of the body. But as the church is subject to Christ, so also the wives [ought to be] to their husbands in everything. Husbands, love your wives, just as Christ also loved the church and gave Himself up for her, so that He might sanctify her, having cleansed her by the washing of water with the word, that He might present to Himself the church in all her glory, having no spot or wrinkle or any such thing; but that she would be holy and blameless. SO husbands ought also to love their own wives as their own bodies. He who loves his own wife loves himself; for no one ever hated his own flesh, but nourishes and cherishes it, just as Christ also [does] the church, because we are members of His body. FOR THIS REASON A MAN SHALL LEAVE HIS FATHER AND MOTHER AND SHALL BE JOINED TO HIS WIFE, AND THE TWO SHALL BECOME ONE FLESH. This mystery is great; but I am speaking with reference to Christ and the church. Nevertheless, each individual among you also is to love his own wife even as himself, and the wife must [see to it] that she reverential obedient and fear her husband." (Eph 5:22-33 NASB)

Wives be "subject" was a Greek military term meaning "to arrange in a military fashion under the command of a leader". In nonmilitary use, it was voluntary attitude of giving cooperation. As a man is to be in subjection under Christ, so it is how God wants a woman to be under her husband. This is not some kind of rude, mean, or better than you think. This is love, life and peace. "For I am the way the truth and life." As a man, my husband is Christ, and he loves me greatly. My husband/Christ wants good for me and wants to give me life more abundantly. Christ is not some cruel, mean husband but a strong loving husband that wants me to trust, adore, obey and honor Him because He wants to love and bless me. If you remember God is love and all his ways are good, then embracing His way you will see His blessings abounding to you and your family. "Come learn of me for I am meek and lowly of heart, and you will find rest for your soul."

Remember that God is no respecter of persons, if you do good you will be blessed but if you don't then sin lies at the door. God is not mocked, if you sow to the flesh, you shall reap a whirlwind but if you sow to the spirit, you shall reap life and peace.

We also see in Ephesians 5: 22-33 that there is even more outlined for the man, so there is more required for him. But we will not investigate this in this book because I will be writing a book devoted to men/husbands later. Let's dig deeper into this reflection of Christ and his church.

"In the same way, you wives, be submissive to your own husbands so that even if any [of them] are disobedient to the word, they may be won without a word by the behavior of their wives, as they observe your chaste and respectful behavior. Your adornment must not be [merely] external-- braiding the hair, and wearing gold jewelry, or putting on dresses; but [let it be] the hidden person of the heart, with the imperishable quality of a gentle and quiet spirit, which is precious in the sight of God. For in this way in former times the holy women also, who hoped in God, used to adorn themselves, being submissive to their own husbands; just as Sarah obeyed Abraham, calling him lord, and you have become her children if you do what is right without being frightened by any fear. You husbands in the same way, live with [your wives] in an understanding way, as with someone weaker, since she is a woman; and show her honor as a fellow heir of the grace of life, so that your prayers will not be hindered." (1Pe 3:1-7 NASB)

We see here also that the apostle Peter is laying out the blueprint for us so that we would be blessed. In verse one we can see the power in a woman being in subjection to her husband. By following this you can cause someone to be won over to Christ without even speaking a word or telling them about Christ, for you will become the living word of God. In verse two we see that way of believing is totally demonized by the world but remember that Christ said you will be hated by the world by following him, you will be spoken of evilly mocked and laughed at. Remember that Christ said don't fear men but fear God, your father who can destroy both body and soul in hell. Christ also said if you love me keep my commandments. In verse 3 we see how He is telling a woman not to be just focused on an outward appearance but to make sure your heart and mind is pure and is shining forth the goodness of God. That a woman should make sure she is bringing forth good fruit that is delightful the ornament of a gentle, quiet and loving spirit. In verse 4 we can see that what's excellent, beautiful, and is very valuable: it is a woman that has a meek & quiet spirit. This moves God. There is a couple of scriptures that explain the opposite woman.

It is better to live in a corner of a roof Than in a house shared with a contentious woman. (Pro 21:9 NASB)

It is better to live in a desert land Than with a contentious and vexing woman. (Pro 21:19 NASB)

A constant dripping on a day of steady rain And a contentious woman are alike; (Pro 27:15 NASB)

He who would restrain her restrains the wind, And grasps oil with his right hand. (Pro 27:16 NASB)

In America and other parts of the world woman are taught that this type of woman is strong, secure, educated and a great prize. This idea of woman that stands up for herself and rules: if a man doesn't like it then society says, oh that man is just scared of a strong and confident woman. When woman act this way it's not beautiful in Gods sight, nor strong or excellent but is actually weak and vexing, it's like smoke in the nostrils. It is no doubt why men want to hide away from woman like this. Here's some examples of a man's response to this: I need to work or go be with his friends all the time or do something so I don't have to be around my wife/girlfriend because I cannot stand being around her.

Let's look at what a virtuous woman is:

"An excellent wife, who can find? For her worth is far above jewels. The heart of her husband trusts in her, And he will have no lack of gain. She does him good and not evil All the days of her life. She looks for wool and flax And works with her hands in delight. She is like merchant ships; She brings her food from afar. She rises also while it is still night And gives food to her household And portions to her maidens. She considers a field and buys it; From her earnings she plants a vineyard. She girds herself with strength And makes her arms strong. She senses that her gain is good; Her lamp does not go out at night. She stretches out her hands to the distaff, And her hands grasp the spindle. She extends her hand to the poor, And she stretches out her hands to the needy. She is not afraid of the snow for her household, For all her household are clothed with scarlet. She makes coverings for herself; Her clothing is fine linen and purple. Her husband is known in the gates, When he sits among the elders of the land. She makes linen garments and sells [them,] And supplies belts to the tradesmen. Strength and dignity are her clothing, And she smiles at the future. She opens her mouth in wisdom, And the teaching of kindness is on her tongue. She looks well to the ways of her household, And does not eat the bread of idleness. Her children rise up and bless her; Her husband [also,] and he praises her, [saying:] "Many daughters have done nobly, But you excel them all." Charm is deceitful and beauty is vain, [But] a woman who fears the LORD, she shall be praised. Give her the product of her hands, And let her works praise her in the gates." (Pro 31:10-31 NASB)

In verse ten it describes the value of this type of woman, and she is worth way more than diamonds so we can see that few women will desire or strive for this. Then we see in verse 11 that her husband's heart trusts in her. You might ask, why? Well, she fears the Lord and is full of his spirit and grace. Therefore, the husband trusts totally in the Lord's spirit that is in her because the Lord says it's not by power or might but by his spirit alone. Even in verse 12 we see the same, she will do him good and not evil. In verse 13 she is concerned with taking care of her family. She is willing and does what is needed to help without being demanded to, she just does it. She does what is needed to bring in food and clothing for her family.

Here's a little joke my mother-in-law, Luann would call from Walmart and ask if we needed anything after she got off work and I would say just have the Simi truck back up to the house LOL. She was acting out of servitude making sure her family had what they needed.

In verse 15 she has a servant's heart which is like Jesus Christ. In verse 16 she is looking how to strengthen her family's financial security. In verse 17 she is strong and determined to be a strength in all aspects for her family. She is courageous and strong in faith. In verse 18 we see what she sells, makes or the job she is doing is excellent. She goes above and beyond to do her best. She has plenty to keep going with her work as her lamp is full. In verse 19 she makes sure her family is clothed just as Christ wants his people clothed with good things spiritually. In verse 20 we can see that she not only cares for her family but that she is also concerned for the poor and needy, she looks to help them also which is also Christ like. In verse 21 she is not scared or worried for winter because her household has warm and good clothing for the winter. In verse 22 she dresses beautifully with clean clothes and looks good for her family. Now in verse 23 let discuss how her husband is known by others: Why? Well, the reflection of Christ is the man, and the reflection of man is his wife so when she shines and is doing great and good in all things and shows such things it causes her husband to shine. She is his glory. What a beautiful thing that a woman can make her husband shine even as the husband makes Christ to shine when he lines up and follows the blueprint. Remember only those who are spiritually minded will see all the beauty, love and freedom in this. Those who are earthly minded or blinded will despise and mock this blueprint. But remember how Christ called some people children of the devil? So, don't be surprised by this because this is also Gods plan to have his children and others that are not His. The children of darkness cannot understand or see the light. That is why we as children of God are to love our enemies. Just as Christ said Father forgive them for, they do not know what they are doing. When people do evil and are blind it's who they are unless God may perhaps grant them a change of heart, mind and cause the light to shine in their heart.

God bought me with his son's blood and filled me with the spirit. I am no longer my own. Just as when we get married, we now belong to your husbands, you are no longer your own. He is now your leader and head.

Chapter 4: Dannielle

If we look back at how the roles of women have changed, especially in American society yet across the world, you see the effects of women's rights and women's liberation. In my opinion this entire movement has had devastating effects on the family but specifically marriage. Both men and women are just not committed to marriage anymore. It is a mindset of well if things don't work out, I can get divorced.

In the 1900's the divorce rate was less than 1%. The current divorce rate is nearly 50%. Now people leave a marriage for a laundry list of different reasons; arguments, lack of commitment, infidelity, lack of intimacy, bad communication, violence, different values, lack of love, financial problems, marring to young, lack of shared interests, just to name a few. What is astounding to me is that 2nd marriages fail at an even higher rate, currently at 67%. I am sure you can imagine third marriages at an even higher rate.

We have strayed from the plan of God for both men and women. God outlines each role, yet we have despised the role God ordained for us as women. We have tried to take on the role of men. There must be positions and roles in any area of life. Ponder this for a minute...you cannot have a ship full of captains. There is an order to things otherwise nothing will ever be accomplished, at least not to the fullness. Who is the leader of this ship? A good captain talks with the crew and listens to them. A leader is only as good as those under him. No one can do anything on their own. If all the men on the ship are captains who makes the ultimate decision? There must be a leader, someone to answer to and lead the crew. Just as we have this example in Christ. He is the head of the body. We are his body as his children. He leads us, corrects us and teaches us. This is the job of a husband with his wife, to lead and guide her to all truth. How can a husband lead his wife if she herself is trying to be a leader above her husband or thinking she is equal to her husband? There can only be one captain, one head of the body. Know your role and place. Stop resisting the order. Women have a great power when we follow the blueprint God so clearly and distinctively laid out for us. We frustrate the grace of God when we try to operate out of our ordained purpose and calling, on our own authority. I fought this very blueprint of God for many years of my marriage with Garrick. I suffered greatly for it and all my family around me suffered too.

    Sharing the reality of what I have done in my life is not easy. Many times, I look back and I am ashamed. Yet I have come to realize that it is because of these trials that I can understand God and His goodness in a different way. Through each struggle and trial, He has brought his word more alive to me. Reading the word of God and the stories are beautiful but when God brings these stories to life with His power and spirit working in your life it becomes part of you because you're living it. In Him we live and move and have our being. On that note here is a life changing story for you.

    I was working nights as a server and Garrick was working days doing construction work. We had our two boys who were young, 2 and 3 years old. I was very unhappy and unthankful with my marriage. I found everything to complain about. I was trying to escape my home life. After work I would think to myself, I am not going home. I was trying to avoid facing my problems. God was drawing out darkness in my heart and I was resisting the change. Through my husband; as God often works this way in a marriage, God was showing that something needed to change in my life and my heart was not right. I have found the spiritual is so often reflected in our actions of our everyday life. Well instead of going home after work to my husband and family, I would go to the bar with the crew I worked with. I was not a drunk, but I was using alcohol to numb myself. I was trying to ignore God and what he was saying to me. I was a mother and wife, but I was neglecting my job given to me by the Lord. I was failing in the calling of God of my life. Garrick was not happy with me of course. After me going out night after night and week after week Garrick confronted me. He was completely reasonable however I was not. When you're in a state of rebellion, trying to go against God's order to things you're not being lead of the spirit and you're operating in your own authority which is never a good thing. Garrick only asked that maybe I would only go out 1 or 2 nights a week instead of 4 or 5 as I had been. He saw how I was neglecting all my home duties. I would be so tired that I was not the mother I should have been either. Garrick petitioned me quite a few times. Time after time I refused. I would try to justify things. He was patient. But after months of this going on he came to me one night when I got home and had printed off divorce papers and signed them. I was devastated. I couldn't believe it. I remember we had a huge argument. I am pretty sure I ripped up the papers. He printed divorce papers two more times. Finally, somewhere in this time God humbled me. I find that sometimes the details of things I can't remember well. I think it's like a trauma you go through in life. Amid this whole time period all I did was cause pain not only to myself but my whole family.

During all of this, we even tried to seek counsel at one point from our pastor and his wife. The counsel we received was horrible. I still to this day cannot believe that they supported me! Another life lesson in that is to be careful who gives you counsel and be sure it matches the word of God.

Praise God in the end I humbled myself and stopped going out so much. I remember after the dust settled from this Garrick told me that he would wait up for me to come home during that period to spend time with me. I was shocked. One of the things I was wanting was for him to pay more attention to me and to have time with him. But I was so bitter and hard hearted that I created more of a separation by my actions. He was trying to meet my needs, and he was doing it right. I was so blinded I could not even see my hands in front of my face. I was so justified in my actions. I was right and he was wrong. In these moments it is truly only by the mercy of God that he gives you eyes to see and ears to hear the truth.

As wife's even if we do not understand why, we must follow the blueprint of God's word. We are given husbands to lead and guide us. As we require our children to obey us and listen to us even if they do not understand. The same with our Lord. Realizing the Lord is always watching out for us, for his plans for us are for good to give us a hope and a future. He does not give us explanations 9 times out of 10. He tells you what to do and you trust and obey. Your actions should never depend on the actions of another. You are accountable to God. We cannot repay evil for evil. My goodness we are commanded to love our enemies! So, we better be loving our husbands that God set over us. We are to reverence and respect our husbands. We are to be helps to them not burdens.

"Do not give your strength to women, Or your ways to that which destroys kings." (Proverbs 31:3 NASB)

"Look at the ships also, though they are so great and are driven by strong winds are still directed by a very small rudder wherever the inclination of the pilot desires." (James 3:4 NASB)

"Can the Ethiopian change his skin Or the leopard his spots? Then you also can do good Who are accustomed to doing evil." (Jeremiah 13:23 NASB)

"I do not nullify the grace of God, for if righteousness comes through the Law, then Christ died needlessly." (Galatians 2:21 NASB)

"The wise woman builds her house, But the foolish tears it down with her own hands." (Proverbs 14:1 NASB)

Chapter 5: The Great General Contractor/Spirit

"Then he said to me, "This is the word of the LORD to Zerubbabel saying, 'Not by might nor by power, but by My Spirit,' says the LORD of hosts." (Zec 4:6 NASB)

There must be the general contractor that oversees the building and makes sure everyone is following the blueprint. Who wrote the blueprint? Well, the father did, and Christ is the engineer, designer, architect, and the general contractor. You then have the foreman, laborers, plumber, electrician etc. Let's look at an example of this in the Old Testament:

"Let them construct a sanctuary for Me, that I may dwell among them. According to all that I am going to show you, [as] the pattern of the tabernacle and the pattern of all its furniture, just so you shall construct [it.] They shall construct an ark of acacia wood two and a half cubits long, and one and a half cubits wide, and one and a half cubits high. You shall overlay it with pure gold, inside and out you shall overlay it, and you shall make a gold molding around it. "You shall cast four gold rings for it and fasten them on its four feet, and two rings shall be on one side of it and two rings on the other side of it. "You shall make poles of acacia wood and overlay them with gold. "You shall put the poles into the rings on the sides of the ark, to carry the ark with them." The poles shall remain in the rings of the ark; they shall not be removed from it. "You shall put into the ark the testimony which I shall give you. "You shall make a mercy seat of pure gold, two and a half cubits long and one and a half cubits wide. "You shall make two cherubim of gold, make them of hammered work at the two ends of the mercy seat. "Make one cherub at one end and one cherub at the other end; you shall make the cherubim [of one piece] with the mercy seat at its two ends. "The cherubim shall have [their] wings spread upward, covering the mercy seat with their wings and facing one another; the faces of the cherubim are to be [turned] toward the mercy seat. "You shall put the mercy seat on top of the ark, and in the ark you shall put the testimony which I will give to you. "There I will meet with you; and from above the mercy seat, from between the two cherubim which are upon the ark of the testimony, I will speak to you about all that I will give you in commandment for the sons of Israel. "You shall make a table of acacia wood, two cubits long and one cubit wide and one and a half cubits high. "You shall overlay it with pure gold and make a gold border around it. "You shall make for it a rim of a handbreadth around [it;] and you shall make a gold border for the rim around it. "You shall make four gold rings for it and put rings on the four corners which are on its four feet. "The rings shall be close to the rim as holders for the poles to carry the table. "You shall make the poles of acacia wood and overlay them with gold, so that with them the table may be carried. "You shall make its dishes and its pans and its jars and its bowls with which to pour drink offerings; you shall make them of pure gold. "You shall set the bread of the Presence on the table before Me at all times. "Then you shall make a lampstand of pure gold. The lampstand [and] its base and its shaft are to be made of hammered work; its cups, its bulbs and its flowers shall be [of one piece] with it. "Six branches shall go out from its sides; three branches of the lampstand from its one side and three branches of the lampstand from its other side. "Three cups [shall be] shaped like almond [blossoms] in the one branch, a bulb and a flower, and three cups shaped like almond [blossoms] in the other branch, a bulb and a flower--so for six branches going out from the lampstand; and in the lampstand four cups shaped like almond [blossoms,] its bulbs and its flowers. "A bulb shall be under the [first] pair of branches [coming] out of it, and a bulb under the [second] pair of branches [coming] out of it, and a bulb under the [third] pair of branches [coming] out of it, for the six branches coming out of the lampstand. "Then you shall make its lamps seven [in number;] and they shall mount its lamps so as to shed light on the space in front of it. "Its snuffers and their trays [shall be] of pure gold. "It shall be made from a talent of pure gold, with all these utensils. "See that you make [them] after the pattern for them, which was shown to you on the mountain. [Exo 25:8-40 NASB]

We can see that God has put in place a simple and beautiful blueprint to follow but we also see he is very precise and detailed in how He wants thing to be. Now let's look at an example from the New Testament:

"He who has My commandments and keeps them is the one who loves Me; and he who loves Me will be loved by My Father, and I will love him and will disclose Myself to him." Jesus answered and said to him, "If anyone loves Me, he will keep My word; and My Father will love him, and We will come to him and make Our abode with him. "He who does not love Me does not keep My words; and the word which you hear is not Mine, but the Father's who sent Me. "These things I have spoken to you while abiding with you. "But the Helper, the Holy Spirit, whom the Father will send in My name, He will teach you all things, and bring to your remembrance all that I said to you. (Jhn 14:21-26 NASB)

Remember that Gods way is perfect and beautiful. He is very merciful and kind so if you find that you have been acting and thinking wrong turn unto him in humbleness and seek His face and plans. You shall live and not only live but have abundant life. Remember it is not by your power or strength but by his spirit. The spirit of God has all wisdom, power, strength and knows all things. So, you may be wondering how this spirit thing works or how do I know if I do have the spirit. Let's investigate these questions. When Jesus was walking with the disciples, he kept saying to them that he must die so we/they could receive the spirit.

"I will ask the Father, and He will give you another Helper, that He may be with you forever; [that is] the Spirit of truth, whom the world cannot receive, because it does not see Him or know Him, [but] you know Him because He abides with you and will be in you. (Jhn 14:16-17 NASB)

Here we see Jesus says that He will ask the father to send the spirit. We then see He says that the spirit abides with them and then tells them that it will also be in them. Let's look at another scripture:

"As for me, I baptize you with water for repentance, but He who is coming after me is mightier than I, and I am not fit to remove His sandals; He will baptize you with the Holy Spirit and fire. (Mat 3:11 NASB)

Here we see John saying he was baptizing people with water for the changing of their minds but a greater one was coming that would baptize them with the spirit and purifying fire. We also see that Jesus said in John 14:26 (NASB), "But the Helper, the Holy Spirit, whom the Father will send in My name, He will teach you all things, and bring to your remembrance all that I said to you."

We see how very important his spirit is, it teaches us everything we need and brings to remembrance everything of God we need. We also see Jesus in John 3:5 (NASB), "Jesus answered, "Truly, truly, I say to you, unless one is born of water and the Spirit he cannot enter into the kingdom of God."

Now let's talk about this, here's after he told them this scripture:

"And behold, I am sending forth the promise of My Father upon you; but you are to stay in the city until you are clothed with power from on high." (Luke24:49 NASB)

We can see that Jesus appeared to them after he was resurrected from the dead.

To these He also presented Himself alive after His suffering, by many convincing proofs, appearing to them over [a period of] forty days and speaking of the things concerning the kingdom of God. Gathering them together, He commanded them not to leave Jerusalem, but to wait for what the Father had promised, "Which," [He said,] "you heard of from Me; for John baptized with water, but you will be baptized with the Holy Spirit not many days from now." So, when they had come together, they were asking Him, saying, "Lord, is it at this time You are restoring the kingdom to Israel?" He said to them, "It is not for you to know times or epochs which the Father has fixed by His own authority; but you will receive power when the Holy Spirit has come upon you; and you shall be My witnesses both in Jerusalem, and in all Judea and Samaria, and even to the remotest part of the earth." (Act 1:1-8 NASB)

He told them to wait till they received power when the Holy Spirit comes upon them. Here we see the Lord telling them He was sending forth the promise of the Father and to wait in the city till they received it. Remember when He was with them in the fleshly body, He told them about the promise of the Spirit, the comforter. Then let's go to the place where they received this power and when they were filled with the spirit of promise:

And suddenly there came from heaven a noise like a violent rushing wind, and it filled the whole house where they were sitting. And there appeared to them tongues as of fire distributing themselves, and they rested on each one of them. And they were all filled with the Holy Spirit and began to speak with other tongues, as the Spirit was giving them utterance. (Act 2:2-4 NASB)

Now here we see and hear of them receiving the spirit and begin to speak in other languages and groanings, declaring the magnificent, excellent, splendid, wonderful, mighty acts of God; as the spirit was moving in them and though them. Now we see many false prophets and teachers have twisted this to belittle it and they usually only use one scripture to deny that this happens when you get filled. Let's look at other scriptures to see the truth. You can quench it as your filled, but you need to yield to it, so it comes out of you with sound.

"For these men are not drunk, as you suppose, for it is [only] the third hour of the day; but this is what was spoken of through the prophet Joel: 'AND IT SHALL BE IN THE LAST DAYS,' God says, 'THAT I WILL POUR FORTH OF MY SPIRIT ON ALL MANKIND; AND YOUR SONS AND YOUR DAUGHTERS SHALL PROPHESY, AND YOUR YOUNG MEN SHALL SEE VISIONS, AND YOUR OLD MEN SHALL DREAM DREAMS; EVEN ON MY BONDSLAVES, BOTH MEN AND WOMEN, I WILL IN THOSE DAYS POUR FORTH OF MY SPIRIT And they shall prophesy. 'AND I WILL GRANT WONDERS IN THE SKY ABOVE AND SIGNS ON THE EARTH BELOW, BLOOD, AND FIRE, AND VAPOR OF SMOKE. 'THE SUN WILL BE TURNED INTO DARKNESS AND THE MOON INTO BLOOD, BEFORE THE GREAT AND GLORIOUS DAY OF THE LORD SHALL COME. 'AND IT SHALL BE THAT EVERYONE WHO CALLS ON THE NAME OF THE LORD WILL BE SAVED.' "Men of Israel, listen to these words: Jesus the Nazarene, a man attested to you by God with miracles and wonders and signs which God performed through Him in your midst, just as you yourselves know-- this [Man,] delivered over by the predetermined plan and foreknowledge of God, you nailed to a cross by the hands of godless men and put [Him] to death. "But God raised Him up again, putting an end to the agony of death, since it was impossible for Him to be held in its power. "For David says of Him, 'I SAW THE LORD ALWAYS IN MY PRESENCE; FOR HE IS AT MY RIGHT HAND, SO THAT I WILL NOT BE SHAKEN. 'THEREFORE MY HEART WAS GLAD AND MY TONGUE EXULTED; MOREOVER MY FLESH ALSO WILL LIVE IN HOPE; BECAUSE YOU WILL NOT ABANDON MY SOUL TO HADES, NOR ALLOW YOUR HOLY ONE TO UNDERGO DECAY. 'YOU HAVE MADE KNOWN TO ME THE WAYS OF LIFE; YOU WILL MAKE ME FULL OF GLADNESS

WITH YOUR PRESENCE.' "Brethren, I may confidently say to you regarding the patriarch David that he both died and was buried, and his tomb is with us to this day. "And so, because he was a prophet and knew that GOD HAD SWORN TO HIM WITH AN OATH TO SEAT [one] OF HIS DESCENDANTS ON HIS THRONE, he looked ahead and spoke of the resurrection of the Christ, that HE WAS NEITHER ABANDONED TO HADES, NOR DID His flesh SUFFER DECAY. "This Jesus God raised up again, to which we are all witnesses. "Therefore having been exalted to the right hand of God, and having received from the Father the promise of the Holy Spirit, He has poured forth this which you both see and hear. "For it was not David who ascended into heaven, but he himself says: 'THE LORD SAID TO MY LORD, "SIT AT MY RIGHT HAND, UNTIL I MAKE YOUR ENEMIES A FOOTSTOOL FOR YOUR FEET."' "Therefore let all the house of Israel know for certain that God has made Him both Lord and Christ--this Jesus whom you crucified." Now when they heard [this,] they were pierced to the heart, and said to Peter and the rest of the apostles, "Brethren, what shall we do?" Peter [said] to them, "Repent, and each of you be baptized in the name of Jesus Christ for the forgiveness of your sins; and you will receive the gift of the Holy Spirit. "For the promise is for you and your children and for all who are far off, as many as the Lord our God will call to Himself." (Act 2:15-39 NASB)

    Here we see as the spirit was filling people that many people were around and heard this all happening and wondered what was going on. Peter starts teaching them by the Holy Spirit what was the meaning of all that was going on and that it was long ago that God told his people that He would pour out His spirit and how it was going to happen. Now we will look at a account of people encountering and receiving the Holy Spirit.

"Now when the apostles in Jerusalem heard that Samaria had received the word of God, they sent them Peter and John, who came down and prayed for them that they might receive the Holy Spirit. For He had not yet fallen upon any of them; they had simply been baptized in the name of the Lord Jesus. Then they [began] laying their hands on them, and they were receiving the Holy Spirit. Now when Simon saw that the Spirit was bestowed through the laying on of the apostles' hands, he offered them money," (Act 8:14-18 NASB)

We see here people that believe in Jesus and even were baptized in the name of Jesus but had not received the spirit. Peter and John went to pray for them and laid hands on them to receive it. We see with common sense that something happened to them especially because Simon the magician asked for this gift because there was something amazing happening that was magical to him and asked for this power and Gift to do what Peter and John did. This would not have been something that the magician would want and be willing to offer money for if it wasn't amazing. Ask yourself why would a worldly person want to buy something that does nothing that he can't see or hear of? Why would he want this if it is like most so called Christians say it is just a feeling or happens, but nothing really happens. We see his heart was evil, but we can also see it wasn't just a touch of the hand or something that wowed people for they were seeing and hearing as in Acts 2 We are seeing the miracle of the Holy Spirit being poured out.

"When Peter entered, Cornelius met him, and fell at his feet and worshiped [him.] But Peter raised him up, saying, "Stand up; I too am [just] a man." As he talked with him, he entered and found many people assembled. And he said to them, "You yourselves know how unlawful it is for a man who is a Jew to associate with a foreigner or to visit him; and [yet] God has shown me that I should not call any man unholy or unclean. "That is why I came without even raising any objection when I was sent for. So, I ask for what reason you have sent for me." Cornelius said, "Four days ago to this hour, I was praying in my house during the ninth hour; and behold, a man stood before me in shining garments, and he said, 'Cornelius, your prayer has been heard and your alms have been remembered before God. 'Therefore, send to Joppa and invite Simon, who is also called Peter, to come to you; he is staying at the house of Simon [the] tanner by the sea.' "So, I sent for you immediately, and you have been kind enough to come. Now then, we are all here present before God to hear all that you have been commanded by the Lord." Opening his mouth, Peter said: "I most certainly understand [now] that God is not one to show partiality, but in every nation the man who fears Him and does what is right is welcome to Him. "The word which He sent to the sons of Israel, preaching peace through Jesus Christ (He is Lord of all)-- you yourselves know the thing which took place throughout all Judea, starting from Galilee, after the baptism which John proclaimed. "[You know of] Jesus of Nazareth, how God anointed Him with the Holy Spirit and with power, and [how] He went about doing good and healing all who were oppressed by the devil, for God was with Him. "We are witnesses of all the things He did both in the land of the Jews and in Jerusalem. They also put Him to death by hanging Him on a cross. "God raised Him up on the third day and granted that He become visible, not to all the people, but to witnesses who were chosen beforehand by God, [that is,] to us who ate and drank with Him after He arose from the dead. "And He ordered us to preach to the people, and solemnly to testify that this is the One who has been appointed by God as Judge of the living and the dead. "Of Him all the prophets bear witness that through His name everyone who believes in Him receives forgiveness of sins." While Peter was still speaking these words, the Holy Spirit fell upon all those who were listening to the message. All the circumcised believers who came with Peter were amazed, because the gift of the Holy Spirit had been poured out on the Gentiles also. For they were hearing them speaking with tongues and exalting God. Then Peter answered, "Surely no one can refuse the water for these to be baptized who have received the Holy Spirit just as we [did,] can he?" And he ordered them to be baptized in the name of Jesus Christ. Then they asked him to stay on for a few days." (Act 10:25-48 NASB)

Here we see Peter was told to go preach the Gospel to the Gentiles (non-Jewish people) which it was not ok to do according to the Jewish ways, so he had to have God come in power and visions to believe. As Peter was preaching Christ Jesus to them, they were filled with the Spirit and the Jewish brothers that were with Peter were amazed and astonished that God would give them the Spirit. They declared they knew this because it was the same way they were filled with the Spirit in Act 2 by speaking in different languages/tongues.

It happened that while Apollos was at Corinth, Paul passed through the upper country and came to Ephesus, and found some disciples. He said to them, "Did you receive the Holy Spirit when you believed?" And they [said] to him, "No, we have not even heard whether there is a Holy Spirit." And he said, "Into what then were you baptized?" And they said, "Into John's baptism." Paul said, "John baptized with the baptism of repentance, telling the people to believe in Him who was coming after him, that is, in Jesus." When they heard this, they were baptized in the name of the Lord Jesus. And when Paul had laid his hands upon them, the Holy Spirit came on them, and they [began] speaking with tongues and prophesying. [Act 19:1-6 NASB]

Here we see how Paul met followers of Jesus and asked them if they have received the Holy Spirit and they said they never heard of this so don't be surprised if you are reading this and that you never heard of this either, don't feel bad. Then we see he asked how they were baptized, and they said by John's baptism. Then Paul preaches to them and then they were baptized in the name of Jesus. Paul then lays hands on them, and the Holy Spirit comes upon them and they speak in tongues/other languages and prophesied.

Here's some more scriptures about the spirit and what it does and what it is good for:

"For one who speaks in a tongue does not speak to men but to God; for no one understands, but in [his] spirit he speaks mysteries. But one who prophesies speaks to men for edification and exhortation and consolation. One who speaks in a tongue edifies himself; but one who prophesies edifies the church. Now I wish that you all spoke in tongues, but [even] more that you would prophesy; and greater is one who prophesies than one who speaks in tongues, unless he interprets, so that the church may receive edifying. But now, brethren, if I come to you speaking in tongues, what will I profit you unless I speak to you either by way of revelation or of knowledge or of prophecy or of teaching? Yet [even] lifeless things, either flute or harp, in producing a sound, if they do not produce a distinction in the tones, how will it be known what is played on the flute or on the harp? For if the bugle produces an indistinct sound, who will prepare himself for battle? So also, you, unless you utter by the tongue speech that is clear, how will it be known what is spoken? For you will be speaking into the air. There are, perhaps, a great many kinds of languages in the world, and no [kind] is without meaning. If then I do not know the meaning of the language, I will be to the one who speaks a barbarian, and the one who speaks will be a barbarian to me. So also, you, since you are zealous of spiritual [gifts,] seek to abound for the edification of the church. Therefore let one who speaks in a tongue pray that he may interpret. For if I pray in a tongue, my spirit prays, but my mind is unfruitful. What is [the outcome] then? I will pray with the spirit and I will pray with the mind also; I will sing with the spirit and I will sing with the mind also. Otherwise if you bless in the spirit [only,] how will the one who fills the place of the ungifted say the "Amen" at your giving of thanks, since he does not know what you are saying? For you are giving thanks well enough, but the other person is not edified. I thank God, I speak in tongues more than you all; however, in the church I desire to speak five words with my mind so that I may instruct others also, rather than ten thousand words in a tongue." (1Co 14:2-19 NASB)

Here Paul is teaching the Church that speaking in tongues doesn't speak to men but to God and he also says when you speak in tongues you edify yourself. We also see he is setting up order in the church, so people just don't start preaching or talking to each other in tongues because it does no good for one another. Especially a new person, they will think everyone is crazy and will not learn anything. We see that Paul also tells the church he will pray in the spirit/tongues, and he will also pray in the understanding; meaning his regular language that he understands. Then he says he will sing in the spirit/tongues and will also sing in the understanding, his regular language.

We can see from these scriptures the huge importance of the spirit and being filled with it. For the spirit intercedes for us because we don't know how to pray as we should, but the spirit does. Therefore, God has always told us it is not by power or might but by his spirit. If you can imagine not having a general contractor to oversee, teach and direct the building of a house! Think of having some people that just know how to nail and cut a board but nothing else. This would end up becoming a disaster. There would be crooked walls, nothing would be square. The foundation would shift and fail. There would be leaks in the roof. The doors would not shut right. Our great God sent His Son to die that he could send forth his spirit to teach, lead and guide us so that our building would be built upon the rock and be a beautiful, stable and sound home which can withstand all the storms of life. This is something to daily walk in and utilize, to be transformed into the perfect man. Remember we are the temple of the Holy Spirit.

Chapter 5: Dannielle

Christ died on the cross that we as His daughters would have access to Him, to have a one on one relationship with him. I thank God that he filled me with his Holy Spirit when I was only 5 years old and gave me a desire to know Him more. One huge key to following this blueprint is to be actively renewed in the Holy Spirit through prayer. Now I know as wife's and mothers we have a lot of responsibilities every day but making time to seek God is key to your salvation and to running a home where the peace and power of God is abounding.

"The wise woman builds her house, But the foolish tears it down with her own hands." (Proverbs 14:1 NASB)

We must daily be renewed in the grace and mercy of God. We need to put on that whole armor of God to be able to stand against the enemy. The enemy wants to stop us from being the women of faith God calls us to be because this is true strength and power as women where we are truly serving God. The devil is no fool, he knows if he stops us as wife's he also hinders our husbands in their callings and causes chaos in home, with our children also.

Something I realized through my husband's guidance is that we all have chains of bondages that need broken in our live's. For me I discovered at a young age that if I did "good" I got a lot less attention from my friends and family. This became a huge negative pattern in my life as I grew up I would do "good" and follow after God and it seemed people weren't "focused" on me so then I would basically purposely do bad to get attention.

At the time I didn't realize this was the case. I would think in my mind well what does it matter no one cares anyway.

So, it became this vicious cycle through my life of going back and forth. It was me being doubleminded which the scripture tells us that a doubleminded man is unstable in all his ways. I would go through these states of depression and feeding negative thoughts and emotions. This led into my marriage. I was basically playing a harlot and sleeping with the devil and then God and back and forth year after year. I was the dog returning to his vomit. I was believing God for a time and things were peaceful in my life and then I would go down a rabbit whole. Things that never bothered me when I was feeding the Holy Ghost where huge issues that I would fight over time and time again. It was always a lust in my members. I wanted something from Garrick that he wasn't doing or giving me. Instead of following after God no matter what my relationship with Garrick was like. I learned your actions should never waver, you must be unmovable in Christ, surrendering all to him.

Truly, Garrick and I have a great relationship when I am walking with the Lord and keeping my focus on him. The sad part is I have thought many times I would get more love or attention by doing it my way instead of Gods way. It is an evil trap of the devil to think we have control. The fact of the matter is you cannot do evil and expect good to come.

I believe that having a true and holy fear of God is key here because your actions are never wavered no matter how people treat you or the circumstances around you. In holy fear you realize the beauty in complete surrender to God. We do not deserve anything good, but we do serve a merciful God that wants good for our lives and relationships. But no matter what you have or don't have your resolve should be steadfast in serving God and doing it his way. You will always have peace in your marriage by making God number one and crucifying your flesh and affections and lusts.

The world will tell you it's okay to speak your mind. Your feelings should be validated. But remember it's not what enters a man that defiles a man but what proceeds out of your mouth. Be quick to hear and slow to speak. We will give an account for EVERY idle word that proceeds out of our mouths.

If you're fighting and arguing with your husband this is of the devil. He comes to devour and separate. God wants husband and wife united in serving him and walking together in his calling for their life. My husband has always told me its's okay to ask questions if a thought comes to you. But you can't believe the devil who is the accuser of the brethren.

I am sure you have had the thoughts ladies, and I included. Oh, Garrick doesn't appreciate me. This is a one that I have feed way too often. The devil knows my weakness here. So, he doesn't tell me thank you for something I did. Here come the floodgates of feelings and emotions. Look he doesn't even care. Yea your right, what the heck???!! I do so much for him. How could he?? Now I have sided with the enemy, and I am serving him, the accuser. If I come to Garrick in this state of mind it will be a fight.

Now the thought comes, Garrick doesn't appreciate you. But if I am in subjection unto God and I am in the spirit, hey babe that made me feel like you don't appreciate me because you didn't thank me for making breakfast. He can now disprove the accusation. Oh no love I am so thankful sorry it's just been a busy morning, and I have a lot on my mind that I need to do for work today. I can now choose to believe him and in doing so side with God or I can refuse. Whatever sure nice excuse! I wouldn't do that to you. This is sleeping with the enemy. I can now side with God and my husband and say okay babe thanks for explaining and we are now united with the Lord walking together. Then this is the end of the matter.

Instead of submitting and surrendering under the authority of my husband I would think I knew better. I went rogue too many times to count and instead of trusting God through my husband's leading and guidance I would follow my feelings. We must realize here feelings come from one of two places. These feelings either feed the spirit of life and abundance or they feed our flesh and the spirit of death and destruction. Therefore, it is so important to be on guard watching and praying always that we are not deceived. And this is our husband's job to help watch out for us as we are the weaker vessel.

I went back and forth day to day or week to week, then eventually month to month, giving place to the enemy and feeding my flesh. God kept teaching me and perfecting me in my heart and mind. The flaw was I gave room to the enemy. We are called to die daily to our flesh as the spirit and flesh are contrary one to the other. I would listen to the lies. Word of knowledge here is that even when what the devil speaks seems "true" it's a lie.

The devil is the father of lies, like seriously he cannot tell the truth. You seriously must be on guard with every single thought that comes into your mind. God started showing me to stop and think where will this thought lead me? What is the end result? How is it making me feel, peace or turmoil? Garrick wrote something years ago that God moved on him, and it has spoken volumes to me. It is based on an old Native American Proverb. I am a firm believer that there is knowledge all around us that relates to God's word and confirms his principals.

> There is a Battle of Two Wolves Inside Us All...
> One is evil. It is anger, jealousy, greed, resentment, lies inferiority and ego. The other is good. It is joy, peace, love, hope, humility, kindness, empathy and truth. The wolf that wins? The one you feed.
> -Cherokee Proverb

Let's relate this to these scriptures...

"Now the deeds of the flesh are evident which are: Immorality, impurity, sensuality, idolatry, sorcery, enmities, strife, jealousy, outbursts of anger, disputes, dissensions, fractions, envying, drunkenness, carousing, and things like these, of which I forewarn you, just as I have forewarned you, that those who practice such things will not inherit the kingdom of God. But the fruit of the Spirit is love, joy, peace, patience, kindness, goodness, faithfulness, gentleness, self-control; against such things there is no law." (Galatians 5:19-23 NASB)

You must choose who you will serve, God or the devil, good or evil. No man can serve two masters. This was my error going back and forth between serving God and serving the devil. I would describe it as a good whiplash after a car accident. I would feed the devil and his thoughts and sometimes it would last 1,2 or even three days was the usual, sometimes even longer. Then it would be like I woke up from a bad dream and suddenly, I could see clearly and all the wrong I had done over the previous days would hit me like a slap across the face. This ALWAYS happened to me when I would resist going to God and falling on my face in my prayer closet. When I would finally surrender and humble myself, God's grace fell on me. Key here is don't kick against the pricks, God resists the proud and gives grace to the humble. A proud and haughty spirit comes before a fall and oh boy have I fallen. But God is full of tender mercies and is not willing that any should perish but that all should come to the knowledge of truth. Beware each day to put on the armor of God that you would be able to stand against the whiles of the devil. Be armed with his armor which is his word, this is your weapon and be clothed with his truth which is life and peace. You are more than a conqueror in Christ, victory belongs to the Lord. Stand with him and he will stand with you. You must have God's grace and mercy upon you. We can do nothing of ourselves, we will always fail and fall short because there is none good no not one. Truly what keeps you submitting to Gods will and plan is His perfect fear. To fear him who can destroy both body and soul in hell. His grace is sufficient for us to perform His will. Realizing here that no matter what anyone else does to us, if your husband upsets you. This does not give you right to act out of your authority as a woman and wife. You must keep yourself in subjection unto Christ's word for it is life and peace. He will take care of the rest, remember his plans for you are always for good.

"For by grace you have been saved through faith; and that not of yourselves, it is the gift of God; not as a result of works, so that no one may boast." (Ephesians 2: 8-9 NASB)

Chapter 6: The Uneducated and Unlearned Novis: "Way of man" and "Heart of man"

Let's look at the ways of man. We see in the beginning man and woman were free to enjoy God in the Garden for they were innocent. Then they went against the Lord's blueprint which was to not eat of the tree of good and evil, but they were free to eat of everything else. We can see the consequences of not trusting in the Lord and his ways.

1) "woman": "To the woman He said, "I will greatly multiply Your pain in childbirth, in pain you will bring forth children; Yet your desire will be for your husband, and he will rule over you." (Gen 3:16 NASB)

2) "Man": "Then to Adam He said, "Because you have listened to the voice of your wife, and have eaten from the tree about which I commanded you, saying, 'You shall not eat from it'; Cursed is the ground because of you; In toil you will eat of it All the days of your life. Both thorns and thistles it shall grow for you; And you will eat the plants of the field; By the sweat of your face You will eat bread, till you return to the ground, because from it you were taken; For you are dust, and to dust you shall return." (Gen 3:17-19 NASB)

Man and woman suffered so much. They were driven out of the Garden and could not freely eat of all the trees. They also were stripped of their privilege to eat of the tree of life which would have allowed them to live forever. Now they would end up dying. We can see how the way both Adam and Eve thought in their minds ended up leading them to hurt, pain, suffering and death. Just as the scripture says that there is a way that seems right to man but it shall lead to death.

"There is a way [which seems] right to a man, but its end is the way of death." (Proverbs 14:12 NASB)

You must exercise yourself in prayer and in the spirit to learn how to decern between good and evil.

"But solid food is for the mature, who because of practice have their senses trained to discern good and evil." (Hebrews 5:14)

Let's remember Jesus said that he was the way the truth and the life. The Light that shines is the gospel and knowledge of God. It says this is eternal life that you might know the father and his son Jesus Christ. If you seek after him you will find him because he is not far from any one of us, but the word is near you, in your mouth and in your heart. If you by faith abide in him and obey his teachings/Blueprint you will have life and life more abundantly. This is a good scripture that has been a huge help for me.

"Therefore, I urge you, brethren, by the mercies of God, to present your bodies a living and holy sacrifice, acceptable to God, [which is] your spiritual service of worship. And do not be conformed to this world, but be transformed by the renewing of your mind, so that you may prove what the will of God is, that which is good and acceptable and perfect. (Romans 12:1-2 NASB)

Chapter 6: Danielle

    Garrick and I were going through a rocky patch. We had just added a wife to the family. On our trip to Mexico a situation arose where I treated my sister wife like I was just talking about in chapter 5. I lashed out on her for something I was feeling which was not even true. This led to a discussion between the three of us. At the hotel pool I told Garrick I think you should spend time in Brazil with our sister wife. We came back home to Colorado and things got worse between us with fight after fight happening. Things need to change with me. Garrick made a stand and said this CAN NOT happen anymore, it is creating turmoil for our family. Garrick ended up spending a month in Brazil and this gave me time to fast and pray. I am thankful God always has had my husband to stand up for righteousness in our marriage no matter what.
    While he was gone that month it was the hardest of our whole marriage for me. I didn't have my head and Lord to help me as I always had before. God had me set a rock outside our home in a specific place to remind me that he is the center of my life, that he is truly the rock that is higher than I, that he is utterly ALL I need in my life. I cannot do it on my own. I will fail. By keeping him my all in all I will inherit everlasting life, no matter the struggles and trials I go through. He loves me and therefore he is perfecting me. I had been putting relationships above serving God. He had not been number one to me.

    We have all been born into sin; all have sinned and come short of the glory of God. As sin entered into the world through Eve, we now are on a journey of perfection in our life's. God sent his son Jesus to die that we can have access to perfection and eternal life. If we as women truly have hearts to know the one and only true God, we will seek daily to know His way because He is our first love.

To truly know God is to be daily seeking His will and for Him to change our hearts and minds to please Him. We all have different struggles. We all have certain things engrained in us from childhood and from life experiences. There are chains of bondages in our hearts that we need Christ to break us free from. But remember, whom the Son makes free is free indeed.

One thing for me has been insecurities and doubt. It is something my mom has struggled with also. Through Garrick's guidance and counsel and the spirit of the living God I have come to the understanding that my confidence is found in Christ alone and it is Him alone that defines me. As God perfects your heart you will also see your marriage strengthened. God will use your husband to teach you. It doesn't mean he himself doesn't have flaws and that God isn't changing him also it is simply the order of things. When you see a fault in your husband you are to take it to the Lord. Reason being is that you are not the head. Christ is the head of your husband and the church, and the husband is the head of the wife. The Lord WILL correct and teach your husband. Your job is not to be contentious and augmentative. We have amazing access to the Lord in prayer. He hears the prayers and cries of his righteous and his ears are open to them all. This doesn't mean you can't talk with your husband about things. It simply means that it should never become and argument when you bring something to Him. It should be peaceable. If you feel your husband is still wrong or not hearing, you then lay it at the Lord's feet. He fights your battles.

Women are the weaker vessel. Eve was the one tempted and drawn away. Our husbands watch for our souls. God wants good for us. We just have to operate according to his will, and He will, without doubt, bless us. Change truly is a beautiful thing but our flesh and spirit are contrary one to the other. Keep seeking for God to burn away any darkness in your heart and to purify your mind.

Let's strive together to enter in at that straight and narrow gate. Let's be women of faith. Let's go back to the principles of God and take our true strength and power back by surrender and being in subjection to our husbands. Let's embrace a meek and quiet spirit.

"To improve is to change; to be perfect is to change often."
-Winston Churchill

"The heart is more deceitful than all else And is desperately sick; Who can understand it? I, the LORD, search the heart, I test the mind, Even to give to each man according to his ways, According to the results of his deeds." (Jeremiah 17:9-10)

Chapter 7: The Disappointments & Failures

Now we will discuss from my life and my wife's life's the disappointments and failures which have happened because of not following the blueprint. I can remember so many failures which lead to so much pain and suffering by not following Gods way. I remember one day God came to me before I started dating Dannielle and God told me that He told Dannielle something and that it was very important. I saw her at church that week. When church ended, I went up to her and told her that God told me that he told you something very important and she looked at me like how in the world do you know about this. I had to ask a few times to get her to tell me. She said that God told her that I was supposed to be with her. That God did not want me with my ex-girlfriend, but I was I was still madly in love with her. Then as she opened her mouth instantaneously a supernatural experience was unfolding before my eyes it was like a bubble surrounded us with God's presence and teleported us to seeing into the future. I was looking at her and, in this moment, she was the most beautiful woman in the whole world we were so in love it was like we had children and we were so happy, and our life was full of peace, love and joy. This all lasted about five minutes then we were zapped back into present time. We both almost couldn't believe what just happed, it was almost like a dream but was real. We both knew that it would be great blessing if we obeyed God, our life would be so blessed.

Now here is where I ran from God's plan. Operating on my own desire, trying to be the head and not submitting to Christ, it was a big screw up. I ended up not listening and going with my own thoughts and ideas thinking and questioning if God really wanted me with Dannielle. Oh, what sorrow and despair I felt as I went on like this for over a year. I keep looking for a better path with my ex thinking maybe God would bless things with my ex. But sorrow and doubt and questions are all that grew. It was such a waste of time and effort just like Jonna and the whale. Finally, I was at crossroads and God made me make a choice to follow him or myself. God spoke to me and said either do it or I will kill your first-born child. I know the spirit was calling me and finally I just surrendered to it and ran full course after the Lord and wow what relief came as I ran after the Lord and His good will. The Blueprint of God is always good and full of peace, joy, and comfort. His ways are always better, and we must trust in Him. Just as a wife must trust in His word/blueprint and God is always faithful to come through.

"But he must ask in faith without any doubting, for the one who doubts is like the wave of the sea, driven and tossed by the wind. For that man ought not to expect that he will receive anything from the Lord, [being] a double-minded man, unstable in all his ways. (Jas 1:6-8 NASB)

I was a double minded man which caused me to be unstable in all my ways. I remember so many empty prayers thinking I was going to change God's mind, how utterly foolish!

"Do not be deceived, God is not mocked; for whatever a man sows, this he will also reap. For the one who sows to his own flesh will from the flesh reap corruption, but the one who sows to the Spirit will from the Spirit reap eternal life." (Galatians 6:7-8 NASB)

If you follow your own blueprint, you will reap corruption and whirlwinds and unneeded sufferings. Turn and follow the only wise and true God and his good and perfect plan and see the goodness of the Lord in your life. Lay your pride and ego down.

God says a very comforting and encouraging way to look at things.

"Let us not lose heart in doing good, for in due time we will reap if we do not grow weary." (Galatians 6:9 NASB)

So, we can see that God is no respecter of persons and if you do it your way it will cause a whirlwind of chaos and pain and sorrow. You can be assured God will not bend or change to your way of thinking. You just have to humble yourself under the mighty hand of God and he will raise you up. He will supply the strength, power, and grace to perform what is pleasing to Him.

Chapter 7: Dannielle

God works in mysterious ways. Thinking back this is one of the most pivotal life stories God wrote for me. I did not realize it then, in fact for years I looked back on this story and distained how God had brought Garrick and I together.

The pastor of the church I grew up going to had family in Colorado. His cousin and her children used to come to Wisconsin and spend most of the summers. One of her daughters and I were close in age. When I was 15 her mom decided to move them to Wisconsin full time. Well, she had a brother. Her brother had a friend named Garrick and he decided to come visit on his Christmas break from college. He was depressed and searching out God. He was reading the Bible hours and hours a day. He ended up staying in Wisconsin and not going back to Colorado. Garrick and I became friends. When I first met him, we both really did not like each other. But as he came to know Christ and I saw him hungering and thirsting after God we began to hang out more and we would talk about God and go for runs together. Our friendship quickly developed. I had a love for him that I had never felt before. I knew he did not view me this way. I knew he was still in love with his ex-girlfriend. I found myself so distraught and in tears all the time that I did not want to hang around him anymore. My mom could see how broken hearted I was. I decided to do a three day fast and prayer about it. I asked the Lord that if these feelings were not from him that He would take them away. I was sure if I prayed hard enough the feelings of love and wanting to be with this man would go away. Then the last day of my fast God spoke to me in my prayer. He told me Garrick is not supposed to be with his ex. He is supposed to marry you. I have put you together. I was like oh yea sure Lord, I am not telling him that he will thing I am bat crazy. So, the next day was Sunday, and we had a church dinner afterwards. Garrick came up to me at the start of church and said the Lord told me you have something to tell me. I was completely shocked!! I even tried to deny it, I was like what do you mean? I don't have anything to tell you. What are you talking about? Garrick was like I know you have something to tell me, the Lord told me. He said let's talk after church. I was like okay. I remember sitting through that church service thinking to myself maybe I can tell him something else. Maybe I can just say I really love you and care for you. I was trying to think of a way out of telling him anything else besides what God showed me. I mean come on there is no way on God's green earth he is going to accept this.

Well after the church service ended and we were all eating together. I remember the whole church dinner I was trying to avoid him. I thought maybe he would forget about it. But the dinner ended, and he did not forget! He came right up to me and said OKAY let's go talk. I was so scared. We went and sat upstairs in an empty pew in the sanctuary. In that moment my mind went blank almost, it was just simple in that second. I opened my mouth and spoke. God told me you're not supposed to be with her your supposed to be with me. As soon as I finished, I thought oh no here it comes he is going to storm off and never talk to me again. As I looked at him tears came to his eyes. He reached in and hugged me and in that moment, it was like nothing else existed. The moment seemed to almost transport us somewhere in the heavenly realm. The love I felt was everything I had hoped and even more. It was the deepest most powerful love I have felt, second to being filled with the Holy Ghost. But even this feeling of love was tied with that same love of the father, it was not of this earth. It was Him flowing in each of us and tying us together with us in him and he in us. It was the three-fold cord. Even as I sit here and recall this moment tears come to my eyes and the Holy Spirit overwhelms me to think of his unending love and faithfulness. There is no greater love than the love of our father and to think he choose Garrick and I to experience the depths of his love together is beyond my human comprehension. I am still in awe of how God wrote our story. I always say He is the best author of all time. The way He writes the stories of our life's is beyond understanding yet at moments we see glimpses of how amazing He is, and in those times, we fall deeper in love with Him, and our roots grow down a little deeper in Him that we would be unmovable and unshakable.

This love story is not the "traditional" one you see in the Hollywood movies it's 100 times better. I used to think why Garrick couldn't have told me. Why didn't you have him fall madly in love with me? You know where I am going with this. I had all the insecurities and doubts. Garrick would always share this story with people of how God put us together. Literally I would cringe inside every time. Sad, I know. To think I thought I could have written the story better than God did. Today I rejoice that he PERFECTLY wrote each detail of that moment. He made zero mistakes and if I had some sort of choice to do it over differently, I would not change a single detail of our love story. Gods' ways are past finding out and past understanding. The one thing I am more assure of than ever is that God loves is the only true love. I am in awe of where he has brought me and where I know he is taking me, to know His love even more.

"I will most gladly spend and be expended for your souls. If I love you more, am I to be loved less?" (2 Corinthians 12:15 NASB)

"keep yourselves in the love of God, waiting anxiously for the mercy of our Lord Jesus Christ to eternal life." (Jude 1:21 NASB)

"Beloved, let us love one another for love is from God; and everyone who loves is born of God and knows God. The one who does not love does not know God, for God is love. By this the love of God was manifested in us, that God has sent His only begotten Son into the world so that we might live through Him. In this is love, not that we loved God but that He loved us and sent His Son to be the propitiation for our sins. Beloved, if God so loved us, we also ought to love one another. No one has seen God at any time; if we love one another, God abides in us, and His love is perfected in us. By this we know that we abide in Him and He in us, because He has given us of His Spirit. WE have seen and testify that the Father has sent the Son to be the Savior of the world. Whoever confesses that Jesus is the Son of God, God abides in him, and he in God. We have come to know and have believed the love which God has for us. God is love, and the one who abides in love abides in God, and God abides in him. By this, love is perfected with us, so that we may have confidence in the day of judgement; because as He is, so also are we in this world. There is no fear in love; but perfect love casts out fear, because fear involves punishment, and the one who fears is not perfected in love. We love, because He first loved us. If someone says, "I love God," and hates his brother, he is a liar; for the one who does not love his brother who he has seen, cannot love God whom he has not seen. And this

commandment we have from Him, that the one who loves God should love his brother also."
(1 John 4:7-21)

Chapter 8: The rebuilding with God's Blueprint

Here's the demolishing of the building so we can rebuild the right way. Here comes the pain the changing of your mind and the humbling of yourselves under his mighty hand that he would raise you up and you would be given the grace to build the right building and be blessed. This will take prayer, forgiveness, love, perseverance, lots of hard work and humility. You will have to die to yourself the world and any other people that will not support you in following Christ and his plan. You will have to be honest with yourself and God. You will have to pray daily and fast often to be transformed into a new creature that has the mind of Christ. You will have to be not conformed to this world but renewed in His will daily. You will need His spirit to lead and guide you with His strength alone.

You will need the spirit of God to kill off the old man and the old way of thinking. You will need to come broken, sad and totally become a person that has no confidence in what you think or want. Cry unto the Lord to lead you as He is the good Shepherd. Have you ever seen sheep? They are ignorant and stupid. They would be run over by a car or eaten by a wolf. They don't even know when the wolf is in sheep's clothing. You need the good Shepard to protect you to lead and guide you so you will need to daily pray in the Holy Spirit because you don't know how to pray as you should, but the Holy Spirit will intercede for you and pray for you. This is not for those that want a quick fix. This is for those that are committed for their entire life. This is going to take a fight and to learn not to listen to the lies in your mind or from other things or people. Remember also God says it is impossible for Him to lie. You can 100% completely trust Him.

"so that by two unchangeable things in which it is impossible for God to lie, we who have taken refuge would have strong encouragement to take hold of the hope set before us." (Hebrews 6:18 NASB)

Remember also God resists the proud but gives grace to the humble. Remember there is a way that seems right to man, but the end result is death. Remember Christ Jesus is the way the truth and the life. He came to give us life and life more abundantly, even in this life. Jesus said come unto me and learn of me for I am meek and lowly of heart, and I shall give you rest.

"Take My yoke upon you and learn from Me, for I am gentle and humble in heart, and YOU WILL FIND REST FOR YOUR SOULS. (Matthew 11:29 NASB)

Remember you can trust the Lord He is good, and all His ways are good. Remember He is the potter, and we are His clay. He will cause you to become separate from people in your life that do not truly support you in following Christ in spirit and truth. This will hurt at times, and you will feel lonely but remember you were bought by the blood of Jesus, and you are not your own. I personally have had God remove people from my life that did not truly support me in following His Spirit. I still pray for those people because I don't know the end result of everything, so I have hope for all I have had the privilege to know.

Even in psychology they have found that the 5 closest people to you in your life you will become like them. Paul the apostle said that bad company corrupts good morals.

"Do not be deceived: "Bad company corrupts good morals." (1Corinthians 15:33 NASB)

Remember also this will take time for healing and restoration just keep the faith pressing unto the mark and high calling that is in Christ Jesus. The right blueprint that needs to be fulfilled will come through the Spirit of God within you and His intercession for you. Remember he is faithful. Remember you are more that victorious in Christ. Remember that God can do far above all you can think or ask. The mighty hand of God is not shortened that it cannot save nor is His ear hard of hearing that He cannot hear.

"Behold, the LORD'S hand is not so short That it cannot save; Nor is His ear so dull That it cannot hear." (Isaiah 59:1 NASB)

"Now to Him who is able to do far more abundantly beyond all that we ask or think, according to the power that works within us," (Ephesians 3:20 NASB)

Remember to fall on the rock and be broken least the rock fall on you and ground you to pieces. Behold the goodness and severity of the living God

"And he who falls on this stone will be broken to pieces; but on whomever it falls, it will scatter him like dust." (Matthew 21:44 NASB)

Just keep yourself moving forward and fighting the good fight of faith that you may be found before the living God with no spot, no wrinkle or blemish but perfect in His love. Now one last thing to lay to heart is don't become unbalanced and become so Holy you destroy your own soul. If you have received insight through this, it doesn't make you to become proud or to think that you are better than anyone but by God's mercy and grace alone He has revealed things to you.

"So, then it [does] not [depend] on the man who wills or the man who runs, but on God who has mercy." (Romans 9:16 NASB)

"For the Scripture says to Pharaoh, "FOR THIS VERY PURPOSE I RAISED YOU UP, TO DEMONSTRATE MY POWER IN YOU, AND THAT MY NAME MIGHT BE PROCLAIMED THROUGHOUT THE WHOLE EARTH." So, then He has mercy on whom He desires, and He hardens whom He desires." (Romans 9:17-18 NASB)

So now as you have learned these things you become no more than a servant.

I would caution you to be very careful the friends you spend time with and the women you seek advice from. Examine the women's life. Is she bearing fruit herself unto righteousness? Is she herself striving to follow these Godly principals? This is especially important when you are young, because you yourself are learning and growing. The more mature you become in the gospel and the stronger your own foundation and walk with Christ is then I believe He will use you yourself to help others. But if someone your around is just continually not wanting to follow these

Godly principals of what God has called a woman to be I would advise you to separate yourself from them.

Chapter 8: Dannielle

When I was newly married and even before I had a friend that was the pastor's daughter. My mom used to tell me that she didn't like me hanging around her and that she thought she was a bad influence. I used to get irritated when my mom said that. If I am completely honest with myself, even then I knew my mom was right. It's hard to be humble and admit your wrongs, but man oh man is humility a beautiful quality in a woman. Her and I were friends for years until God had Garrick and I move with our sons to Colorado. That period in my life brought so much spiritual change. It is wild to me that when God does not want someone in your life he removes them and then there have been seasons also when people come back into your life. God knows exactly what you need in each season.

"You are the average of the five people you spend the most time with."
-Jim Rohn

"Older women likewise are to be reverent in their behavior, not malicious gossips nor enslaved to much wine, teaching what is good, so that they may encourage the young women to love their husbands, to love their children, to be sensible, pure, workers at home, kind, being subject to their own husbands, so that the word of God will not be dishonored." (Titus 2:3-5 NASB)

I was in my friend's wedding and for part of her gift to her bridesmaids she gave each of us a framed photo of the two of us together from her bachelorette party. When the point came that I knew she would not be in my life of course I was saddened greatly, she was in my life for nearly 30 years. God gave me a vision; I was looking at this picture sitting on my dresser at the time and time fast-forwarded. Her and I were posing for a picture together, but we were old. It gave me peace, hope and comfort, because more than anything I hope to share eternity with her. I rejoiced that our story together is not over. We are just not what each other needs in this time and season of life. Key here is to trust God's plan for your life always, even if it's painful because in sorrow the heart is made better.

" 'For I know the plans that I have for you,' declares the LORD, 'plans for welfare and not for calamity to give you a future and a hope." (Jeremiah 29:11 NASB)

Let us join as women of faith, women of honor, women of integrity, women who love the Lord first and foremost in their life's. Let's be lights in darkness, let's not be ashamed to stand out in a world where being a submissive wife is considered weak. Do not be deceived my sisters, God is a God to be feared and reverenced. His way is the only way. If you want to honor God and gain everlasting life, if you want a good marriage while you're here on this earth the key is following the blueprint.

"For I am confident of this very thing, that He who began a good work in you will perfect it until the day of Christ Jesus." (Philippians 1:6 NASB)

Chapter 9: The Peace, Joy & Contentment

Oh, the benefits of the God of Love are past understanding, joy overwhelming, comforting the soul, peace past understanding, a contentment and a clean conscience before him. These benefits are better than sex, better than drugs, better than money, better than any earthly thing imaginable. His love and presence are the most intimate and comforting thing that you will ever experience. Let's look at some experiences people had with the Lord and his presence.

"A Psalm of David, when he was in the wilderness of Judah. O God, You are my God; I shall seek You earnestly; My soul thirsts for You, my flesh yearns for You, In a dry and weary land where there is no water. Thus I have seen You in the sanctuary, To see Your power and Your glory. Because Your lovingkindness is better than life, My lips will praise You. So, I will bless You as long as I live; I will lift up my hands in Your name. My soul is satisfied as with marrow and fatness, And my mouth offers praises with joyful lips. When I remember You on my bed, I meditate on You in the night watches, For You have been my help, And in the shadow of Your wings I sing for joy. My soul clings to You; Your right hand upholds me. But those who seek my life to destroy it, Will go into the depths of the earth." (Psalms 63:1-9 NASB)

"Then he said to them, "Go, eat of the fat, drink of the sweet, and send portions to him who has nothing prepared; for this day is holy to our Lord. Do not be grieved, for the joy of the LORD is your strength." (Nehemiah 8:10 NASB)

"Open the gates, that the righteous nation may enter, The one that remains faithful. "The steadfast of mind You will keep in perfect peace, Because he trusts in You. Trust in the LORD forever, For in GOD the LORD, [we have] an everlasting Rock." (Isaiah 26:2-4 NASB)

When Elizabeth heard Mary's greeting, the baby leaped in her womb; and Elizabeth was filled with the Holy Spirit. And she cried out with a loud voice and said, "Blessed [are] you among women, and blessed [is] the fruit of your womb! "And how has it [happened] to me, that the mother of my Lord would come to me? "For behold, when the sound of your greeting reached my ears, the baby leaped in my womb for joy. "And blessed [is] she who believed that there would be a fulfillment of what had been spoken to her by the Lord." And Mary said: "My soul exalts the Lord, And my spirit has rejoiced in God my Savior. "For He has had regard for the humble state of His bondslave; For behold, from this time on all generations will count me blessed. "For the Mighty One has done great things for me; And holy is His name. "AND HIS MERCY IS UPON GENERATION AFTER GENERATION TOWARD THOSE WHO FEAR HIM. "He has done mighty deeds with His arm; He has scattered [those who were] proud in the thoughts of their heart. "He has brought down rulers from [their] thrones, And has exalted those who were humble. "HE HAS FILLED THE HUNGRY WITH GOOD THINGS; And sent away the rich empty-handed. "He has given help to Israel His servant, In remembrance of His mercy, As He spoke to our fathers, To Abraham and his descendants forever." And his father Zacharias was filled with the Holy Spirit, and prophesied, saying: "Blessed [be] the Lord God of Israel, For He has visited us and accomplished redemption for His people, And has raised up a horn of salvation for us In the house of David His servant-- As He spoke by the mouth of His holy prophets from of old-- Salvation FROM OUR ENEMIES, And FROM THE HAND OF ALL WHO HATE US; To show mercy toward our fathers, And to remember His holy covenant, The oath which He swore to Abraham our father, To grant us that we, being rescued from the hand of our enemies, Might serve Him without fear, In holiness and righteousness before Him all our days. "And you, child, will be called the prophet of the Most High; For you will go on BEFORE THE LORD TO PREPARE HIS WAYS; To give to His people [the] knowledge of salvation By the forgiveness of their sins, Because of the tender mercy of our God, With which the Sunrise from on high will visit us, TO SHINE UPON THOSE WHO SIT IN DARKNESS AND THE SHADOW OF DEATH, To guide our feet into the way of peace." (Luke 1:41-79 NASB)

"They said to one another, "Were not our hearts burning within us while He was speaking to us on the road, while He was explaining the Scriptures to us?" (Luke 24:32 NASB)

Here's an encounter I once had with the Lord; I was spending time with him praying for a couple of hours. I was praying a lot in the spirit. I was on my knees lifting my hands up in the air and my eyes were closed, then I opened my eyes, and I was inside a pure blue fire. It was not hurting me but as I would pray in the spirit it would cause the blue fire to grow more intense. There was so much joy, peace and love, it was overwhelming. Remember that as you abide in His teaching's/blueprint there will be the reward for walking this way because it is impossible for God to lie. For if you sow to the spirit, you shall reap life and peace everlasting.

I know from experiences when I have followed the teachings of Christ and followed the leading of the Holy Spirit that my life has been so blessed. I have seen the Lord continually bless me and my family in every aspect doing miracles, blessing beyond what I could have ever imagined or thought of. It did not all come easy. I have had to leave many friendships. I had to leave my fathers and mothers and brothers and sister for Christ and the move of the spirit. Remember this, that Jesus said that your enemies will be those of your own household and a prophet is not welcome among his own family. But they did not want me to follow the spirit and wanted me to deny the Lord and to please them and not God, but thanks be to God for his amazing grace to be able to overcome and follow Him and not to please man.

Chapter 9: Dannielle

When I was 4 years old our pastor's son was also 4. One church service I saw him get filled with the Holy Ghost and start speaking in an unknown tongue. I remember just watching him as he prayed and was overcome. I left that church service with a hunger for God. I wanted to be filled with the presence and power of God. I wanted that too, it lit a fire in me!

I knew in my heart I needed this. I think a few months past. I was at home with my mom, and she was doing dishes in the kitchen. I said to her mom I want the Holy Ghost. I remember she looked at me and said OKAY well let's pray. She put on some worship music, and we knelt in front of the couch. My mom started praying in the Holy Ghost and she grabbed my hand, and she said all you have to do is speak. As she started speaking in tongues it was like I could feel an overwhelming heat from her hand that transferred into my body. I opened my mouth, and in that moment, I was filled with the Holy Ghost and started speaking in an unknown tongue. I will never forget that feeling, I did not want it to end.

God filled me with his amazing love and power when I was 5 years old and he has guided me day by day since then. I cannot imagine my life without the power of His spirit in me and flowing through me. In the same way I cannot image my life without Garrick as my husband and Lord. Through him God has perfected me year after year. God joined us together because he knew I needed someone to lead and guide me. I am so thankful for God blessing me with a man that is truly after His own heart. I trust completely in God and therefore I trust Garrick because I see Christ continually working in him.

    As a woman I have learned the importance above all else of a relationship with the Lord. For he leads us and guides us to all truth. Think of it like this, if someone told you buy a lotto ticket with these numbers, go to this location and buy the ticket and you will win. Would you follow the steps? What would you have to lose? Nothing...go thy way as thy faith makes thee whole. What do you believe? Choose today who you will serve.

    We are not our own! Especially once he meets us and fills us with his sprit. He laid out a plan of salvation in his word and it does not just stop, it is a continuation through your life of living your life to please him. We are on a straight and narrow path to gain life eternal. There is a way to follow and an order to things.

" 'I am coming quickly; hold fast what you have, so that no one will take your crown." (Revelations 3:11 NASB)

    Life is short here on earth. Use each moment wisely. I hope to see you in heaven my sisters. I petition you to serve the Lord and to do this you must serve your husband as your Lord. God did not make a mistake and there are no loopholes. So, if you have been trying to get around this and find some other way, let me be the one to tell you I have tried all the other ways, and they don't work. Don't learn the hard way. I did that for you already. Please heed my warning because suffering due to your stubbornness and disobedience just makes things worse. I pray for each of you my sisters, that God would give you a willing heart to know him for he is neigh to you.

"Concerning this I implored the Lord three times that it might leave me. And He has said to me, "My grace is sufficient for you, for power is perfected in weakness." Most gladly, therefore, I will rather boast about my weaknesses, so that the power of Christ may dwell in me. Therefore I am well content with weaknesses, with insults, with distresses, with persecutions, with difficulties, for Christ's sake; for when I am weak, then I am strong." (2 Corinthians 12:8-10 NASB)

"For though we walk in the flesh we do not war according to the flesh, for the weapons of our warfare are not of the flesh, but divinely powerful for the destruction of fortresses. We are destroying speculations and every lofty thing raised up against the knowledge of god, and we are taking every thought captive to the obedience of Christ, and we are ready to punish all disobedience, whenever your obedience is complete." (2 Corinthians 10:3-6 NASB)

Remember God is called mans helper and so are we, so we have a great and Nobel calling.

God will honor you by following his way! Remember whose daughter you are. Fight the good fight my sisters.

Closing

The amazing thing is that God sets up situations in our life and especially in a marriage to see what you will do. Then depending on what you do it will bring destruction or life and peace. Remember the flesh and our ways are contrary to the Lord and his spirit. Bring this to remembrance because I pray and want you to receive life, peace and joy in your marriage and especially with God. Remember daily to pray with your whole heart in the spirit and your understanding, sing in both also, for God inhabits the praises of his people. In doing this you will receive the grace to overcome the ways of the world and will receive the power to obey God and walk in His good and acceptable will for your life.

Remember, be of good courage and be strong because the scripture says let us not lose heart in doing good for in due time, we will reap benefits if we don't grow weary. Trust me, God is faithful, and His mercies endure forever. He will bless those who follow His teachings, for His power is past understanding. He is a great God that created the heavens and the earth and all things on the earth including you.

I pray in the name of Jesus Christ, that God's grace would abound to you, that you may fulfill all His ways and that the light would shine in your hearts and minds, that you may shine forth his glory and righteousness. I pray that you may comprehend his will and ways. May God's peace abound unto you with His mercy that is in His son Christ Jesus.

Your friend and brother in Christ Jesus and your sister,

Garrick and Dannielle

www.ingramcontent.com/pod-product-compliance
Lightning Source LLC
Chambersburg PA
CBHW020753230426
43665CB00009B/575